DEDICATION

I dedicate this book to my two daughters Kelly Gibson and Sally Mulready. And also my two daughters-in-law, Lainey Staires and Lisa Staires. Also my granddaughters Meg, Molly, Sophie, Gracie, Madisson and Clare. As well as all the wonderful women who have touched my life through the years! You know who you are!

My Sincere Appreciation for:
Simone for typing the manuscript
Georgia for editing & preparing
Mike and Lainey for proofing
The Medical Team at Saint John's Hospital
For helping me to restore my life
The Lord for inspiration and desire to
Keep on keeping on!
Thank you team!

ENDORSEMENTS

It's hard to find words to express my gratitude for my mother-in-law, Shirley Staires. She has been a faithful mentor to me from my teen years and on into marriage and motherhood. I am blessed! If ever a person needs a hug, an encouraging word, or a loving exhortation to soar to the heights of all God has created you to be, she's just the woman to talk to! She has been my inspiration to live life to the fullest; to humbly learn about the gift of who I am and all that I possess with confidence. She is a teacher and a student, a giver and a gift.

-Lainey Sanders Staires

Shirley Staires has given her life to ministry primarily to mentoring women. She can hear from the Lord and act as a vessel to pour forth into women. All of life is about "telling the next generation of the wonders of the Lord and how He desires to use each one of us for His Kingdom." May this book be utilized to train and equip you to pass it on to the next generation.

-Kelly Staires Gibson

I love your new book, "A Symphony of Words from A to Z." You are giving sweet melody to my everyday life. I love your heart and your passion and the way you reach out to women in our community. I know this book will be a daily inspiration filled with scripture and wisdom for women everywhere.

-Lisa Jenson Staires

Rare in life do you find a committed warrior of the Lord, more passionate about souls being saved and lives pursuing abundant kingdom living, than Shirley Staires. Shirley's life picture is one of "daily walking out the Kingdom of God," and all that means. She has successfully found words to help us build the foundation to live abundantly, and the bridge to help others live abundantly.

-Sally Staires Mulready

A

Symphony of Words From A to Z

To Help Orchestrate Your Life

———— ◆ ————

Choose the melody you want to sing by

choosing your words for the day.

Let the music begin...

THE ALPHABET SONG

A you're adorable

B you're so beautiful

C you're a cutie full of charm

D you're a darling and

E you're exciting and

F you're a feather in my arms

G you look good to me

H you're so heavenly

I you're the one I idolize

J We're like Jack and Jill

K you're so kissable

L is the love light in your eyes

MNOP I could go on all day

QRST alphabetically speaking you're ok

U make my life complete

V means you're very sweet

WXYZ It's fun to wander through the alphabet with you…

To tell you what you mean to me!

(Music by Sid Lippman and lyrics by Buddy Kaye. 1940-1955)

Word from the Author: As I was writing each word, many songs would come to mind. Because of copyright laws, I chose not to include songs other than the song listed above – The Alphabet Song sung by Perry Como   (and a fun song to sing). Perhaps you will also be reminded of melodies being orchestrated in your hearts as you read. Who knows, you may even write a new song, symphony or melody.

CONTENTS

PREFACE

I suppose every author has hopes and desires that their book will make a profound difference in the reader's life; or it will light a fire in someone who has grown cold or lukewarm in their closeness to Christ. I'm no different! This book started out to be words of encouragement to close friends and women in the weekly classes in my home. I felt a momentum developing as I wrote each word, then began adding a prayer and declaration to action. I suddenly realized the alphabet has 26 letters and that could easily be a monthly word encouragement book.

I desire for this book to be used as a "call to arms;" an inspiration to fuel your fire to action; a melody that keeps reminding you to get in sync to the melodies of action that the Lord is writing today for we women. This book is not only a beautiful book to possibly be used as a devotional book, but to induct you into a strong company of women being armed for battle today.

Motivation words on each page are written to enlist you to join forces with other women (young and old), to rise up in your chosen destiny today. Inspiring words to motivate you, prayer to guide you, and the Holy Spirit declaration to empower you. That is why this book is written...to help you join hearts with other women to develop strategies the Lord is calling forth today.

A strategy has been used against we women long enough. I'm called to destroy and defeat the enemy to expose his exploits against us. Prayer, faith, declaration and agreement of God's Word will defeat all the lies and attempts. We women are arising! Do you hear the trumpet sounding? I'm calling forth an army of women to select their weapons of words to combat all the strategy of the enemy...especially the lies. If the praise team and musicians were sent forth to lead the battle, lets choose our weapons of words to help orchestrate our lives and win!

Miriam took a tambourine in her hand (and all the

women followed her) with tambourines and dancing and sung the song of victory to the Lord. When was the last time you took a tambourine and led other women to sing and dance, rejoice together for how the Lord has brought you through troubled waters?

> *"I will sing to the Lord for He has triumphed gloriously, the horse and riders thrown into the sea. The Lord is my strength and my song, He has become my salvation."*
> *Exodus 15:1-2*

> *"Sing to the Lord, for He is highly exalted..."*
> *Exodus 15:21*

Anonymous, Abound

The word Anonymous can happen when our potential is unseen and our abilities are unappreciated! Ever feel like that? So many things happen in our lives that we don't have answers for at the time, but later on, it can have great meaning. Only proving that God's stewardardship of

> *"There is a season (a time appointed) for everything and a time for every delight and event or purpose under heaven."*
> *Ecclesiastes 3:1 AMP*

our lives is a mystery. He can use every circumstance and event (both difficult and great)! Most of us agree it's the most difficult times that

1

drive us to the heart of our Father and these become our greatest growth times.

> *"The Lord your God is with you, the Mighty Warrior who saves. He will take great delight in you; in his love he will no longer rebuke you, but will rejoice over you with singing."*
> *Zephaniah 3:17 NIV*

Prayer:
Father, thank You that there is a time and season in my life where You orchestrate a beautiful symphony. Even when I'm not hearing the melody. I abound to the sound of music dancing all around me. You sing over me through all my seasons and the melody lingers on....

Jesus constantly spent time with His Father to be reminded of who He was and the mission He was to bring forth on the earth. Only a third of His life was spent in ministry, while the other 90% was hidden in anonymous times of preparation. Preparation that included working in the carpentry shop; obedience to His parents; in the wilderness; and preparation for His purpose! If it was necessary for Jesus to endure the things He suffered, the same will apply to us who choose to follow Him! Allowing His grace to be sufficient is a gift we must learn to receive over and over.

Abound means *pressed down and running over with blessings from Heaven!* It is when you are overwhelmed at the grace and glory of the Lord. The times He surprises you by giving you wells you didn't dig; property you didn't even ask for; overwhelms you with His love and presence; giving you running-over favor with Him and others!

> *"And God is able to make all grace [every favor and earthly blessing] come in abundance to you, so that you may always [under all circumstances, regardless of the need] have complete sufficiency in everything [being completely self-sufficient in Him], and have an abundance for every good work and act of charity."*
> *2 Corinthians 9:8 AMP*

> *"You crown the year with Your goodness, and Your paths drip with abundance."*
> *Psalms 65:11 NKJV*

Some call it "lucky," but to those who have learned to trust the Lord in every situation, it is totally amazing grace. Let's learn how to surrender to both of these invitations! Have an abounding day even if you are hidden in the shadow of the Most High and feel anonymous! If His shadow is

there, then He must be close!

Prayer:
Lord, thank You for your abounding presence in me! You
are the greater One living within me and the One who
causes me to abound in Your abundant provision. I lack
for no good thing. You have taken up residence within me
and supplied me with every good and perfect gift. I am full
and running over-ready to do Your will! I am not
anonymous but chosen for such a time as this!
Amen

> I declare that because the Lord has promised me an abundant
> life, I choose to receive this and actively claim it for every
> member of my family-**now** and for generations to come. We
> will each choose to believe, receive and follow Jesus Christ - we
> consistently walk in His ways. Through every season of life,
> whether anonymous or exalted, we find contentment, rest and
> protection in the Father who delights in us. We have complete
> sufficiency in Him with an overflowing abundance in every way.

ACTION STEPS:

✍ What does this mean to me?

✍ What must I do?

Beautiful

Oh Lord, You're beautiful! You created a beautiful world for us to live in. Just as sin polluted the Garden, we have polluted this beautiful earth with our own ideas, selfish ways, and the devaluing of people, places and things. We have called evil good, and good evil. There are many that things You created and said were beautiful—feet, garments, humans, the Temple, flocks, crowns, the washing of feet, holiness, grace and Your Beautiful Bride (meaning we who believe). We've been deceived in our own ignorance...but we repent! We realize we have sinned against You and what You Lord, intended for good.

We sing about America the Beautiful and truly it is, but I want to offer a challenge to those of us who choose to believe that we are the ones who make it beautiful. We tend, maintain, correct, weed, beautify, and do our part on the outside, but I believe the Lord is after the hearts of His people. He is concerned about the thoughts, attitudes, and false belief systems that lurk in the hidden recesses of the heart. These are the ones the Bible speaks of as pretenders or hypocrites; those who clean

> *"The Spirit of the Sovereign Lord is on me, because the Lord has anointed me to proclaim good news to the poor. He has sent me to bind up the brokenhearted, to proclaim freedom for the captives and release from darkness for the prisoners, to proclaim the year of the Lord's favor and the day of vengeance of our God, to comfort all who mourn, and provide for those who grieve in Zion— to bestow on them a crown of beauty instead of ashes, the oil of joy instead of mourning, and a garment of praise instead of a spirit of despair. They will be called oaks of righteousness, a planting of the Lord for the display of His splendor."*
> Isaiah 61:1-3 NIV

the outside, but within they are full of extortion and self-indulgence. In Matthew 23:25 Jesus gives a strong word to first clean the inside of the cup before the outside! He values content above appearance so no more white-washing! It's wonderful to look beautiful on the outside, but God's priority for us are clean hands and a pure heart. This is what and who the Lord is looking for. Time to be real! Time to get free of any pollution, scum, stinkin' thinkin', and self-will. Don't you love being around someone who is

> *"Behold, how beautiful you are, my darling, behold, how beautiful you are! Your eyes are dove's eyes."*
> *Song of Solomon 1:15 AMP*

just downright good inside and out? It is so freeing and fun just to be with them. You might want to re-read Matthew 23 as a reminder. How about being a BA today! And what is that? A Beautiful Ambassador! You are officially crowned to bring beauty wherever you plant your feet. No more functioning as legalistic, judgmental believers – also known as *religious spirits.*

9

He has made everything beautiful in its time - so IT IS TIME! Time to turn our lives around to the goodness and beauty that God has created in us. No more pretending; no more trying to look good and impress. Instead, let's accept the truth of where we are and make a commitment to be conformed into the image of Christ. Let this transformation be evident in our hearts, our homes, our neighbors, our church, and to the world!

Everyone is looking for the real deal! If you have been looking for realness, and are fed up with those whose hearts are still trying to prove themselves, then you be the one to set the example as a vessel and prove the love of God. Be the one whose heart has been strangely warmed by the Holy Spirit; the one who has been in the presence of the One who is love personified! You be the one who knows and walks in the beauty and love of Jesus! Yes, the time is now my beautiful one! (CAUTION: Do not try to do this on your

own by glossing over, justifying or waiting on other
Believers to go first! Be the forerunner in your family,
group, and church to step up and obey! You are the
miracle waiting to happen so others will have courage
to try!) This is what is called, living in the Kingdom of
God "on the earth as it is in Heaven," loving God and
loving others!

> Prayer:
> Father, I am grateful to belong to You knowing You make
> all things beautiful – including me! The time is NOW for
> me to trust Your promise over me, that I am fearfully and
> wonderfully made. No one else in the world compares
> with me. I'm unique, filled with potential that is not
> compared to any other. I am gifted, talented, and
> strategically alive for such a time as this in the world. My
> destiny is ready to be released. It is for this time that I was
> born.
> Amen

I declare that You are beautiful Lord, and because your Spirit lives
in me, Your glorious beauty shines through me. I proclaim the
freedom, favor, and comfort that Christ's sacrifice provided me. I
receive a crown of beauty instead of ashes; joy instead of mourning
and a garment of praise for a spirit of despair. I am a former
captive set free! I choose to reflect your glory more and more each
day!

ACTION STEPS:

✍ What does this mean to me?

✍ What must I do?

Chosen

Being chosen is such an awesome experience! Remember the times in your life when you were waiting to be chosen? Chosen to participate in a very prestigious ceremony; chosen as a bride, or perhaps the most terrifying of all...will I be chosen to be on the team with my peers (especially in grade school, junior and senior high school). Then there was the Prom...oh my,

> *"You did not choose me, but I chose yo and appointed you so that you might go and bear fruit— fruit that will last..."*
> *John 15:16 NIV*

what about a date for the Prom? As we grew up, we still had great anticipation that we would be asked to serve, be the speaker, or be chosen and recognized for whatever great deed we had done.

Then came the most important decision of our life: Would I choose to follow Christ? Would I be willing to forsake my own choices, my own life and choose to totally yield my heart to His call for my life? And that was only the first question! Since then, you are constantly being called to surrender

> *"But if serving the Lord seems undesirable to you, then choose for yourselves this day whom you will serve, whether the gods your ancestors served beyond the Euphrates, or the gods of the Amorites, in whose land you are living. But as for me and my household, we will serve the Lord."*
> *Joshua 24:15 NIV*

more to become more like Him and give up your reputation, your opinions, and your carnal desires. You are the CHOSEN ONE! You are finding out that bearing fruit is a Call! Your search has got to be to find out what that looks like for you! Exploring what kind of fruit you are called to bear is an adventure! What delicious fruit are you called to develop to its full maturity? Will it be with children, men, women, in the Church, outside the church, in your business, to your city or to the nations? Will it be to those who need to rebuild their lives, or to disciple new Believers? Is it Risky? You bet! That's why you have to stop and evaluate what you say "yes" to. However, YOU ARE CHOSEN! Only the Holy Spirit can truly teach you and develop you fully to bear fruit that will last. Remember you

> *"I have been crucified with Christ and I no longer live, but Christ lives in me. The life I now live in the body, I live by faith in the Son of God, who loved me and gave Himself for me."*
> *Galatians 2:20 NIV*

were chosen out of the world to follow Christ! He wants to get the world out of you as well. That's why we come to Him to be with Him to become as He is! Yes, it's a Miracle...crucifying the flesh, allowing the old you to die!

Joshua made this choice for his whole family, whole household. He said, "As for me, and my house, WE WILL SERVE THE LORD!" If you have said this over your family, most likely you are waiting for them to get the message! Some hear and obey immediately. Some watch your life to see if it changes anything. Some still desire their own choice and lifestyle! But you and I, because we love our family and want the very best life for them, cry out to our Father to not forget our household! We desire for them to experience what He is giving to us...freedom, wonder, fulfillment, purpose, destiny, peace and miracles! It's not a life without trials and challenge, but a life with grace and power to overcome when they do come fully into following Christ.

So, choose Christ this day! Make your choice to not just wait and See! But Make your choice to choose to be chosen by the Christ of Calvary, perhaps the greatest word starting with "C"!!! Let the Love of Christ CAPTURE YOU today!

Prayer:
Father, the best choice I ever made was to choose Christ! To become more like Him every day. Thank you Holy Spirit for leading and guiding me daily to remember to allow you to change me into Christ's likeness.
Amen

I declare like Joshua, "As for me and my household, we will serve the Lord, and Him only will we serve." Now each member of my family has the responsibility of making their own choice. However, I declare life and blessing over each person to choose wisely whom they will serve. Today is the day to know you are chosen and collect your Promised Inheritance!

ACTION STEPS:

✍ What does this mean to me?

✍ What must I do?

Delight

Remember the day when America was the land of delight and all the nations called us blessed? Remember what an honor it was to be recognized as the Home of the Brave and the Land of the Free? Remember what honor, truth, integrity, and freedom stood for? Remember how we all desired to walk in these truths, and teach our children that this is what we believe? When the people of this nation would choose

> *"And all nations shall call you happy and blessed, for you shall be a land of delight...says the Lord of Hosts!"*
> *Malachi 3:12 AMP*

to obey God and walk in His ways? Remember when the Constitution was written and the government was filled with men of integrity whose hearts were for following God as they governed the people? On this day when we remember those freedoms, my heart remembers and rejoices!

I have 82 years of remembering my county's heritage and the thrill of watching a Parade of Honor as we witnessed the servicemen and women march behind the American flag, standing as we sang the Star-Spangled Banner as the guys removed their hats with honor. We wept as we remembered the wars of the past and for those who gave their lives for us. I remember during WW2, we kept a light burning in our window as a reminder to pray for God to bring our service men home safe.

Teachers, preachers, CEOs, employers, employees, students, mom, dads, all Americans, we don't need to just remember those times, we are the ones to make

America a delight in this generation! Ask yourself today, how can I make America a land of delight? How can I bless America?

May I make a few suggestions to help jog our memory? Love God, reach out to be kind, loving, helpful, truthful, patient, observant, neighborly, friendly, steadfast in what you believe. Be ready to defend truth at any cost; make wise decisions, worship God, be a watchman, be happy and if you're not, then get happy! Follow Christ and simply do what He did by reading His life story found in the Bible! Love children and protect them at any cost. Love your family! Dads, be the best and moms, outdo your family with love! Kids, straighten up and fly right! Simply do what's right and only run with those who do! Choose your friends, your mate, your belief system v-e-r-y carefully! It will determine your future!! Your words are powerful; use them wisely and never to bring harm. Be quick to judge yourself and even quicker to repent! Learn the joy of choosing to be a servant and living a life of quiet unseen deeds! This makes the Lord smile in delight!

It's hard to lead where you won't go, and hard to be what you don't know! Time to change all of that if you are longing for delight! The best way to do this is to:

> *"Delight yourself in the Lord, and He will give you the desires of your heart!"*
> *Psalm 37:4 NIV*

Okay, time for the desires of our hearts to be met. But we gotta get ourselves in the right positions to receive. July 4th is America's Day of freedom so let's make it our day as well! Come on Americans, we've been robbed! Let's bring back that good ole patriotism, love for our country, honor and respect for one another, obedience to our parents and the laws of the land! Let's fly the grand ole

> *"...if my people, who are called by my name, will humble themselves and pray and seek my face and turn from their wicked ways, then I will hear from heaven, and I will forgive their sin and will heal their land."*
> *2 Chronicles 7:14 NIV*

flag once again. Take back whatever prevents God from blessing our land of delight! Ready? Go!

Prayer:
Father, we are standing fast declaring our love and allegiance for the land of America that we love so dearly. We bless America, even though we have such division, separation, no understanding for one another. Children against parents, protestors against our government, racial inequality, denominational divisions, country against country and people in the streets demonstrating against police shootings. Because we love America, we bless and ask our God to bless America. Do we deserve His blessings? No, but His mercies far outweigh our lack. We cry out for freedom to ring out repentance and rain your delight and favor over us Lord as we fall on our knees, humbly before you!
Amen

I declare to speak and choose delight rather than depressed. I choose enjoyment, pleasure, acceptance, rather than defiance or deficiency (lack of appreciation or honor). Delight makes me happy, full of joy, expectant for God's Best for me! I choose delight over discouragement! I fully expect to be delighted, in awe, and amazed at His Love over me!

ACTION STEPS:

✍ What does this mean to me?

✍ What must I do?

Encourage

To encourage one another...to me, that means *everyone* who crosses my path (that I meet or even think of) each day. Plan and prepare for divine encounters along the way! Let your heart be overflowing with the joy and goodness of the Lord - especially if you don't feel like it. It's contagious! There are those who are waiting for you to come along so don't miss it. Ask the Lord who needs a prophetic, encouraging word and be ready to give

> *"But encourage one another daily, as long as it is called "Today," so that none of you may be hardened by sin's deceitfulness."*
> *Hebrews 3:13 NIV*

it! Prepare yourself for the day by reminding the Lord you are available and at His service.

There are Believers we are called to encourage and bless each day! You are just a blessing waiting to overflow! How do we do this? Let me count the ways...a telephone call, email, letter, card, or prayer. Consider a lunch date, invitation to your home, or meeting for coffee. Don't forget to speak a word to a total stranger.

> " Let us seize and hold tightly the confession of our hope without wavering, for He who promised is reliable and trustworthy and faithful [to His word]; and let us consider [thoughtfully] how we may encourage one another to love and to do good deeds, not forsaking our meeting together [as believers for worship and instruction], as is the habit of some, but encouraging one another; and all the more [faithfully] as you see the day [of Christ's return] approaching."
> Hebrews 10:23-25 AMP

The Lord loves to see His family gather together just for the fun-of-it! Assemble, gather, but above all ENCOURAGE! It's not only good for your health and well-being, but the

Lord seems to delight in it! Because where we are...He is! Always be prepared to give a Word in season!

> *"But in your hearts revere Christ as Lord. Always be prepared to give an answer to everyone who asks you to give the reason for the hope that you have. But do this with gentleness and respect, keeping a clear conscience, so that those who speak maliciously against your good behavior in Christ may be ashamed of their slander."*
> *1 Peter 3:15-16 NIV*

Everyone needs a blessing!

Prayer:
Lord, help me to be "on assignment" every day to give an answer and a blessing for the hope that is within me. Let my eyes see who needs a blessing' and let my ears hear what you would like to speak over someone. Let my mouth be quick to speak that encouragement. Amen

---

'I declare that I will encourage others! Many words can be used to speak to others. I choose to encourage and only use words to build up and overflow with kindness. Words in season to speak to a person's Spirit within.

ACTION STEPS:

✍ What does this mean to me?

✍ What must I do?

Father

What is the role of a father? In today's modern family, the father doesn't always have the best image. Society has its own idea of fatherhood.   Because every important role for the family has been lessened today, we have confusion, absence, brokenness, loss, and a longing for a father's love and protection. Some call it

"Not everyone who says to me, 'Lord, Lord,' will enter the kingdom of heaven, but only the one who does the will of my Father who is in heaven."
Matthew 7:21 NIV

an "orphan spirit:" when one doesn't feel loved or cared for. When one feels alone without purpose or direction.

When one feels abandoned, lost in the crowd. When one feels he doesn't have what it takes to measure up. God created fathers to impart this blessing! God is calling for Fathers to have His heart so that men know how to be courageous men; and women know the value and honor of being a woman.

Jesus knew this feeling as well! His Father planned for him to come to earth and bring forth His Kingdom on the earth! His Father had a plan for him to follow step by step. That is why Jesus continually pulled away from the crowd to seek His Father's

> *"For those who are led by the Spirit of God are the children of God. The Spirit you received does not make you slaves, so that you live in fear again; rather, the Spirit you received brought about your adoption to sonship. And by him we cry, "Abba, Father." The Spirit himself testifies with our spirit that we are God's children. Now if we are children, then we are heirs—heirs of God and co-heirs with Christ, if indeed we share in his sufferings in order that we may also share in his glory."*
> *Romans 8:14-17 NIV*

Will. Others could not give answers, and even his disciples were asked to pray and trust the Father to comfort and guide Him as He was called to finish His

30

time on earth. Only Father God could give to Him what he longed for in that hour.

So, what does this tell us as we live our lives on the earth? It has driven me to the Father's heart for what is needed in me to enter the Kingdom of Heaven. If you are (or were) blessed with your earthly Father's love and blessing, then you are a truly blessed child. If you weren't, then like me, you have had to search for that blessing. Thank God for His Holy Spirit who finally captured me and convinced me that I belonged to my Heavenly Father and that He truly had a plan for my life on the earth. His Will? Yes, I seek His will every day, and sometimes I feel His pleasure and presence in the process! Even when I don't feel it, I still seek. I am hopeless, helpless and undone without His victorious right hand to lift me up where He is!

In His Presence is joy forevermore! Only in that space do I feel His favor and grace surrounded by His love! Surrounded by God's earthly family who love to lavish hugs and words of encouragement-this is when I know I am in my Father's Will. Don't you want to live there? Nothing like feeling the Father's pleasure and delight.

> Prayer:
> Thank you Father that we have You! You created and destined us to be part of Your family. We belong! Give me your heart Father; a heart to love like You.
> Amen

I declare the Father's heart to be released over families. A divine outpouring throughout the earth. May fathers bend their knee and hear from Father God how to love their wives and their children and how to love and accept themselves. I declare a rising up of families in the Lord because fathers are taking their spiritual positions in the family, in the church, at work and community. Fathers arise! A revival of fathers today!

ACTION STEPS:

✍ What does this mean to me?

✍ What must I do?

Glorious, Greatness, Glory and Grace

The world would be a very gray colorless place to live

if it wasn't for all the

glory of God which we

see each day with the

varied colors of

creation (the sun,

moon, skies, green

earth, trees, and

> *"All together now—applause for God! Sing songs to the tune of his glory, set glory to the rhythms of his praise. Say of God, "We've never seen anything like him!" When your enemies see you in action, they slink off like scolded dogs. The whole earth falls to its knees—it worships you, sings to you, can't stop enjoying your name and fame."*
> *Psalms 66:1-4 MSG*

gardens of color.) Who cannot marvel at the brilliant

colors of birds, animals of the sea, leaves, and the glistening colors of lakes and rivers?

Then you add the supernatural power of the Shekinah Glory that at times comes to reveal the presence of Jesus. How we love those times when we feel the breath of

> *"They are new every morning; great is your faithfulness."*
> *Lamentations 3:23 MSG*

God and the rushing winds of the Spirit. Added to all

> *"Holy, Holy, Holy is the Lord of hosts; the whole earth is filled with His glory."*
> *Isaiah 6:3 AMP*

that glory, is His glorious grace. Those times when His amazing grace reminds you how He found you when you were

lost without hope. When He protects you from a bad decision or bad accident. Yes,

> *"So whether you eat or drink or whatever you do, do it all for the glory of God."*
> *1 Corinthians 10:31 NIV*

those times when we say, "I've never seen anything like what He can do!"

Remember the book we all love, *Hinds Feet on High Places?* At the end of the book the Lord changes the names of Sorrow and Suffering and Much-Afraid. He reminded them that His name for them was Joy and Peace, Grace and Glory! What a difference a day makes when you truly see yourself the way God sees you. He will change your name as well – just ask Him!

> *"Love is to be sincere and active [the real thing— without guile and hypocrisy]. Hate what is evil [detest all ungodliness, do not tolerate wickedness]; hold on tightly to what is good."*
> Romans 12:9 AMP

Prayer:
Father, thank You for sending Jesus, our great and glorious King of Kings! Thanks to Jesus for displaying His glory wherever He went. His grace was amazing! Never had people heard such a message of love and grace – a new thought process called The Kingdom. If this was His way to live and love, then why do we not totally choose to live it? Perhaps because our minds cannot comprehend such love; a love too marvelous to believe. And yet, it's not only the more excellent way--it's the only way!
Amen

I declare the whole earth to be released to show forth the Lord's glory. We behold Your glory Lord in heaven and the beauty of the earth. Now may Your glory be released in Your people. May we shine like stars. May Your glory and grace be so fully released in Your people that the earth will marvel at our love for grace and kindness knowing it is the glory of the Lord bringing the Kingdom.

ACTION STEPS:

✍ What does this mean to me?

✍ What must I do?

Hidden

The Hebrew word yada means to come together; to intersect; to intertwine your life closely with the Lord; to weave the Bride and Bridegroom closely together. It seems for us to know the mysteries of God, namely Christ, we must find the hidden treasures of wisdom and

> *"For you died [to this world], and your [new, real] life is hidden with Christ in God."* Colossians 3:3 AMP

knowledge. In order to seek and find these treasures, we must also hide ourselves in Him!

I have been gaining a greater understanding lately of the importance in knowing what it means to be

"Hidden in Christ." There are times to be on the visible front line of what God is doing, and then there are times when you find yourself being called as an "undercover agent," not to be seen. You may be called to see the strategy more clearly and be led away from the main battle. Jesus, (our commanding officer) calls us to come away with Him to hear His heart, His tactics, and be assured we are hearing His voice clearly. Much like Jesus had to pull away from the crowd to hear His Father's voice to discern His next steps. I realized that 90% of Jesus' life was spent hidden in the wilderness, and in the background to prepare Himself for the task set before Him on earth.

We have learned our lessons well here in America! We are #1 and must lead the pack! We have the answer and must place ourselves in a position to be heard. We sometimes misunderstand the call to be hidden and resist with all our might, as though we are the answer and must be present to lead!

Only our Father knows the motives of our hearts, and at times He just wants to connect with us to remind us of His love, and what He is calling us to be for Him. We sometimes feel that

> *"His brightness is like the sunlight; He has [bright] rays flashing from His hand, and there [in the sunlike splendor] is the hiding place of His power."*
> *Habakkuk 3:4 AMP*

we must be up front to be seen and heard, but He is

> *"And you, my son Solomon, acknowledge the God of your father, and serve him with wholehearted devotion and with a willing mind, for the Lord searches every heart and understands every desire and every thought. If you seek him, he will be found by you..."*
> *1 Chronicles 28:9 NIV*

saying, "Come away my Beloved! I have treasures for you that can only be found hidden in Me." And we say, "Show me Your Face Lord, let me hear Your Voice! I need Your touch, Your presence and Your assurance. I run to You Lord to be in that glorious hidden place alone with You!"

So, as He calls and beckons unto us, let us hear and run to Him to find that hidden place where He dwells. Allow Him to restore that hidden place in our hearts! It brings Him great delight to have His own sheep listen and respond to His Call. May we be totally changed and transformed in that hidden place with Him!

Prayer:
Father, I love when you call unto me as your maiden so fair. It reminds me I am chosen and you hear my prayer. Bless me Father, as I seek the greatest treasure of Your love in the hidden places of Your Kingdom.
Amen

I declare that the hidden places of the enemy will be exposed. The times when we have been deceived by the coming of the accuser. I declare and disclose now the hiding places where the enemy has beguiled God's people. I speak now! Turn on the brightness of our glory Lord; reveal our own hearts where we have believed a lie. May we rise up out of the hidden places we have retreated to and shine God's light courageously to expose and diminish any strongholds that would prevent the full exposure of God's plan. We are sheep and we only hear the voice of the Shepherd. A strange voice we will not follow.

ACTION STEPS:

✍ What does this mean to me?

✍ What must I do?

Identity

As preposterous as this sounds, it must be true or it would not have made it into our Bibles. Can you believe that our standing in the world is identical with Christ's? To me that means He has made me just like Him. I not only represent Him in this world, but I have His nature, His power, His ability, and I behave like Him! His language is my language. My image is truly in His image!

There's only one way for this miracle to happen. When we give the Holy Spirit permission to not only live, but rule in us, this gives us the nature and power that allows us to love and be like Jesus. I'm working on that, how about you? This is part of our mission...to prove to the world that Jesus is alive and lives in us!

If you were arrested today for loving Jesus, would there be enough evidence to convict you? (Just had to use that phrase from long ago)! Let this mind of Christ be in you. Let Him overwhelm you with His love and empowerment so not only the world will know, but you will be overcome by His overflowing life in you that is so much bigger than you! That's when you say OMG, this is for real!

> "God is love. When we take up permanent residence in a life of love, we live in God and God lives in us. This way, love has the run of the house, becomes at home and mature in us, so that we're free of worry on Judgment Day—our standing in the world is identical with Christ's. There is no room in love for fear. Well-formed love banishes fear. Since fear is crippling, a fearful life—fear of death, fear of judgment—is one not yet fully formed in love."
> I John 4:17-18 MSG

Make it happen! Don't look in the mirror for proof, check out His Word and see if you are bearing fruit like Him! Being in His image and

48

knowing your identity is in Him, you will literally drip with honey and be covered with God's Favor. He loves His Son in you! He recognizes Jesus in you, when He sees how you love! Now that's a loving Father!

Prayer:
Father, Jesus knew exactly who He was and His purpose for coming to the earth. He left us a great example to follow. If I am uncertain who I am in Christ and how I'm to function for the Kingdom, I can totally miss what I was born for. Continue to reveal to me how You have purpose and destiny for my life. I especially thank You for freely pouring Your love into me so I can freely pour it out to others. It's a love that will not let me go!
Amen

I declare my true identity in Christ! I am saved, redeemed, filled with the Holy Spirit and power; in my weakness His power is made perfect. His power released in me can bring healing, deliverance and set people free. The same power that raised Christ from the dead now dwells in me. He has freely given me all that He was and is, so that His power is released in me to totally change the world. I carry only good news of the Kingdom and am on a mission to deliver this throughout the world. I will not fail! Christ in me can do all things well. I must constantly remind myself what Jesus sees in me and how Heaven looks at me! Fulfilling the Purpose I was born for ~ and knowing my full identity in Christ! I will not accept any negativity!

ACTION STEPS:

✍ What does this mean to me?

✍ What must I do?

Jesus

When Jesus sees us here on earth, He does not recognize our age, weakness, doubt, fears, inability, culture, race, position, history of our broken family, sin, iniquity, past, unbelief, wrong choices, hurts, failures, secrets, hiddenness, sickness, handicaps, separation, mourning, depression, heaviness, hopelessness, addictions, or anything else that you think you are! He doesn't see any lies that have held us down throughout our lives that may have kept us from the truth of who we really are! He is searching over the world to find those whose hearts truly love and believe in Him. Those who are fully persuaded that we are loved and accepted in Him and have chosen to rise up and believe! Willing to serve Him with hearts of abandon! He only sees what's missing and wants to replace the darkness with light!

It is just as if Jesus sees you as His very own; His masterpiece, His warrior, His bride, His righteousness, His ambassador, His child, the one He died for, the apple of His eye, as forgiven, as His sheep, His strength and song, the one He has put His trust in. Jesus see you as the one He hears when you call; His chosen for a special purpose and destiny; the one He loves to hang out with; the one He will never leave or forsake; His child who will never be orphaned; the one He has poured His favor over, healed, delivered, and set free.

Jesus speaks to you as His beautiful one. The one He brings to His banqueting table. His banner of love waves over you as a protecting and comforting anointing. Jesus sees you as one who calls upon Him freely and runs to Him as the hiding place. You are His Lights in this world, a beacon that invites all who dwell in darkness. You are His intercessor who helps others in distress, and the one who is daily filling your lamp with oil, eagerly awaiting His coming! Above all, He sees you as captured by His love and filled with His amazing grace forever and ever!

Now, what were you saying about regrets and complaining about what's missing in your life and where you fall short? Perhaps it would be wise to "think like Jesus thinks!" Dare to believe His Word about you. If He says you are fearfully and wonderfully made, and that He is your Creator, then perhaps He holds the truth! Whose report will you believe?

Yes, you are a champion, highly favored, and born to be part of His royal family! Knowing this and choosing to walk in it, takes a humble, childlike, willing, and very grateful spirit! This would be YOU! Choose to live the way Jesus sees you! The days I choose to remember and believe this truth are glorious days, just as He promised!

From Isaiah 61 (AMP), just a few things that need replacement from bad news to good News – why not think a new thought:

FROM BAD NEWS	TO GOOD NEWS
Meek, poor and afflicted	Gospel of good tidings
Brokenhearted	Healed
Mental/spiritual captives	Liberty and freedom
Bound	Opening of prison doors
Bad Year	Proclaim it is an acceptable year
To all who mourn	Consolation and joy
Ashes	A garland of beauty
Mourning	Oil of joy
Heavy burdened, failing spirit	Garment of Praise, strong, magnificent, lofty oaks of uprightness, justice and right-standing with God! You shall be called the Priests of the Lord - people will speak of you as ministers of God, you shall eat the wealth of the nations, and the glory shall be yours!
Shame	Two-fold return.

Dishonor and Reproach	Rejoicing in what you are given. Receive double what you gave up
Robbery/violence	God hates wrong with violence, He will give recompense in truth and will make an everlasting covenant with them. Their offspring shall be known among nations and the people who see them in My goodness will recognize and acknowledge that they are the people whom the Lord has blessed. Turned from wicked hearts to hearts after God, ones with a different spirit.
No longer covered in Sin	You are clothed with the garments of salvation, the robe of righteousness. The Lord will cause rightness and justice and praise to spring forth before all the nations through the self-fulfilling power of His Word!

That's the real Replacement Theology of Jesus! Now choose to believe it for you and your household and let the Kingdom of Heaven take over! It's all about Jesus, yall! For it is in Him we live and move and have our being.

Prayer:
Jesus, You have totally captured me with Your love and grace. No one could ever love me like you! Your lovingkindness is never ending. Your mercies are new every morning. Your call upon my life gives me purpose and destiny. Your promise for me is everlasting abundance of life. You are my all in all Lord! How can I not be forever grateful and full of praise? Your face is all I seek and Your presence is always and forever with me.
Thank You Jesus!
Amen

Not only the sweetest Name I know, but the most powerful word in my whole vocabulary! He is my all; my everything; my total reason for living! He is Lord of my life, the One I live for, the Overcoming One, and the Son of God who died on a Cross, shed His Blood to remove my sins; my Lord and Shepherd and soon-coming King of Kings and Lord of Lords! And I'm one of the ones Jesus Loves!

ACTION STEPS:

✎ What does this mean to me?

✎ What must I do?

Kingdom

In order for the Kingdom to come on earth as it is in Heaven, looks like you and I are the answer! We pray for His Kingdom to come on the earth, and yet, He says, "It is within us!" Since we can't give what we don't have, and we can't tell what we don't know - perhaps it is time for us to "Seek the Kingdom within" to fully preach, teach, live and enjoy what we possess! Jesus came to earth to reveal and live the Kingdom of Heaven! Everything He did pointed to what the Kingdom looked like...what He did, what He spoke, how He lived! He always pointed to and proclaimed His Kingdom as He preached - this was His message! This message has somehow been hidden throughout the ages, and seldom preached, and yet, the Kingdom was His message that He longed for us to receive!

If you check out your concordance in the back of your Bible, and look up Kingdom, there is a very long list of Kingdom references found in your Bible. If you choose to look each one of those up, and choose to relate and activate Kingdom in your own life, then you will know fully what the Kingdom looks like and how to live it. And wise you will be in our Father's eyes!

So, this is my challenge to you today, (if you choose to accept it)...according to Matthew 6:33 SEEK FIRST HIS KINGDOM (over anything you need, what to eat, what to wear, where to go, who to see, or any worries about tomorrow). When we get the atmosphere/attitude of the Kingdom, we see Jesus in a brand new way! His revelation to us is so much more defined, focused, and direct.

I have spent the last 20 years at least, seeking His heart for the Kingdom, and I feel like I've only just begun! Now I'm taking others with me throughout the City looking for His Kingdom in operation. When we find it, we rejoice and celebrate! When we don't, we pray and declare it over that place and people! For more information, look up Mathew 6:33, and for some real adventure, go on your own search to find His

> *"...nor will people say, 'Here it is,' or 'There it is,' because the kingdom of God is in your midst."*
> *Luke 17:21 NIV*

Kingdom. If you walk in order, peace, abundance, righteousness and joy, you've found it. It is within you! Now you must go forth teaching, preaching, proclaiming, and prophesying: The KINGDOM OF GOD IS AT HAND! If Jesus is present then His Kingdom has come.

Prayer:
Our Father who art in Heaven, Hallowed be Your Name.
Thy Kingdom come, Thy will be done on earth as it is in
Heaven. Now give us this day, our daily bread. Forgive us
our trespasses, as we forgive those who trespass against
us. Lead us not into temptation, but deliver us from evil.
For Thine is the Kingdom, the power and the glory forever!
Amen

I declare this kingdom of righteousness, peace, and joy is being
released throughout the earth. I choose to do this by teaching,
training, preaching, healing, raising up disciples to go into all the
world, every mountain of society. Take the name and power of Jesus
and purposely go forth to set captives free. Jesus said the fields are
white for harvest. I feel compelled to teach, train, send forth disciples
to the harvest field. I declare it knowing it shall done!

ACTION STEPS:

✍ What does this mean to me?

✍ What must I do?

Lavish

Most likely, you can recall a time in your life when you felt so much love, you could hardly put into words how that made you feel. Whether you had just won or achieved something, or perhaps done nothing. You may have felt very alone and even unloved. Then a wave swept over you that you

> "See what great love the Father has lavished on us, that we should be called children of God! And that is what we are! The reason the world does not know us is that it did not know him."
> I John 3:1 NIV

could not explain...a wave of favor and love that exalted you to a higher place. You couldn't figure out what you had done to deserve this wonderful feeling! And yet, though feeling undeserving, you felt great reward! Indescribable really! This is a picture of lavish...when we receive generously from our Father! What a wonder when we receive something we totally didn't expect.

The word Lavish means very ample or generously! Or, how about slather? This seems to be what the Holy Spirit is doing today...seeking out and finding ones to lavish (or slather) God's love upon! Even in our sin and rebellious nature, Jesus is drawing and loving us to Himself. After all, it was for us that He died and is longing to lavish His Love over us in very generous portions. We are chosen, set apart as His people, called according to His purpose and desire! I urge you, encourage you, and call you, to respond to the Shepherd's voice. Rise up and follow! Sure you have scars, hurts, wrongdoings and perhaps wrong choices you have made. It's time to come out from under that shadow/veil that presses you down. Time to come out of your self-centeredness and gather up your baskets to be filled to overflowing! Simply lay down that old woe-begone spirit and stand up ready to receive your lavish supply from your Father! When we consider the level of love that would cause Jesus to go to the cross for us, don't you think that might qualify for lavish? Talk about giving generously! He willingly laid down His life for you and me. If it's a vast supply,

> *"In him we have redemption through his blood, the forgiveness of sins, in accordance with the riches of God's grace that he lavished on us. With all wisdom and understanding,"* Ephesians 1:7-8 NIV

then I call that lavish supply! Plenty enough for all!

Prayer:
Father, we sure could use some of your lavish supply today! So, right now, we pour out a lavish supply of our love over You, and ask for Your lavish supply over us! We're running low and truly need an overflowing generous infilling! And because You overflow us, now we have plenty to lavish over others! Thank You Father when we ask - we receive, in Jesus' Name.
Amen

For those who have never sensed or experienced this lavish love, let me encourage you right now to simply ask our heavenly Father to pour His generous supply of love over you. Nothing can compare! It's like a warmth flowing over you like warm oil. Although supernatural, it remains forever! Jesus died for this love to be poured over us to embrace and empower us to love others like He loves us. You know it's real when you can't wait to share with others. Oh, how He loves you and me!

I declare this day that the lavish, overabundant love of Jesus is being released throughout the earth. As needs get greater and hearts get heavier, His lavish love is ready to pour buckets of love and gladness over His family. The Father's love is more than enough for His children, but we have forgotten to ask. Ask, therefore, that your joy maybe full to overflowing. Lavish in His presence, His joy is unspeakable and full of glory!

ACTION STEPS:

✎ What does this mean to me?

✎ What must I do?

Man with a Maiden

One of the most beautiful sights in all the world is to see a man with a maiden whom he is pursuing and longing to know better. Whether it's a little boy in Kindergarten who can't stop chasing a little girl on the playground; or a teenager who is falling all over himself trying to figure out how to ask a girl to go get a Coke; or the man who has found the one he loves and is continuing to pursue her toward marriage. The girl loves to be pursued, and the man loves to pursue! When this is pure and holy in the Lord, 'tis a beautiful thing! He was born to protect, and she loves being protected. He knows how to hear God's voice. She knows how to hear and follow that voice.

God said in the very beginning, "It is not good for a man to be alone, but to come together in covenant and bind their hearts together as one." Paul says in the Bible that this is truly a miracle! After pursuing, comes the perfecting of the relationship to become one. This can take a lifetime! Many a couple determine that this is taking way too long and choose to break it off

> "There are three things that are too amazing for me, four that I do not understand: the way of an eagle in the sky, the way of a snake on a rock, the way of a ship on the high seas, and the way of a man with a young woman."
> Proverbs 30:18-19 NIV

in the process! The real miracle takes place for those who choose to stay and allow love to have its full effect. This truly takes the Holy Spirit to teach, train, humble, give orders and bring heaps of courage to both the man and the maiden. The dating relationship can be exciting, the moving towards marriage can be hazardous, the wedding itself can be glorious, and then comes the marriage!

Ah, a man with a maiden is a work in progress, especially when the Lord is Lord over the couple and both hearts longing to follow the Lord and not give up until that Oneness is achieved! A deeper understanding is that you are created equal (no hierarchy, or superiority over each other) and both should desire to exalt one another to the highest position God has planned. Help one another to be the best you can be (with no competition or race to the top). I believe marriage is a beautiful thing when the Lord is conforming and transforming each of the couple to their greatest fulfillment. Honor, respect, hope, and helping each other to please the Lord, oh what a miracle blessing! This is what love looks like in its purest form. The man lays down his life for his wife, and his wife respects him fully, outwardly, publicly! She learns what it means to refresh and comfort him, and he convinces his maiden that of all the women in the world, he has chosen her and she surpasses all others. That my friend, is what God intended for a man with a maiden!

I have been young, and now I am more than young (ha), and this is my story! I know the love of a teenage boy, who later became the love of the man I married. I'm all for love and marriage, but only if you have learned the joy of being a servant. Loving and serving each other means losing yourself in God's Love. It's the only way! I do hope you experience this love in your life. Then your love expands to all those kids, grandkids, extended family, friends, and all those brothers and sisters in Christ! But it all starts by loving God with all your heart, choosing to follow Christ in His love, and allowing the Holy Spirit to empower you to live this life of love! I believe this is what Kingdom love looks like! Or maybe it all starts by watching a man with a maiden and asking God to allow you to experience this personally in your life. Life is not perfect on the earth, but God can sure give us a taste of Heaven when our relationships thrive and grow in His love! WARNING: It can be risky! Requires death to your flesh! But oh, the joy it brings!

Prayer:
Father, I pray for every maiden to receive these words from our loving Father, our Savior Jesus or the Holy Spirit. Every girl and woman I know needs to know she is pursued. To think You would purposely pursue the maidens You love with this longing of Your heart is what every female needs to experience. May all we maidens recognize Your desire to live within us and never allow Your love to grow cold.
Amen

I declare two declarations for maidens. That maidens with hearts after God will rise up today in the fullness of knowing who we are in Christ. Fully prepared, fully empowered, fully pregnant with God's desires for such a time as this. And that we would have the courage of Deborah, Esther, Mary the mother of Jesus, to fulfill God's request for them in their generation. Then you take Joan of Arc, Rosa Parks, and mighty spiritual women...leaders of today whom God is using so mightily. Women, God is requiring a dedicated courageous heart among His maidens today...do you hear the call? I declare you not only hear, but are rising up to obey!

The second is this. . .I declare there is a new revelation being poured over godly men today in the Body of Christ, for how mightily the Lord wants to use women today. There are gifts and callings in women that men were never intended to complete. Men have authority! Women have influence! Women are being prepared in strong influential ways to turn the hearts of kings' to change and birth laws in the land today to bring life. I declare it in Jesus' name. I pray for an army of men to stand up for Women today to honor, support, accept as God's anointed for specific leadership. Wise is the man who has eyes to see God's Plan and Purpose for using women mightily throughout the ages. And may we women stay humble, knowing our identity in Christ and not feel an need to prove ourselves. Humility and contentment will elevate us as we trust in God! And men, this begins with how you treat your wife!

ACTION STEPS:

✍ What does this mean to me?

✍ What must I do?

Name

We have come to realize the importance of names and the meaning of them. When we discover what our name means, it can bring clarity and identification as to who we are. Whether the one who named us realized the spiritual meaning or not, we carry a name that can help us discover our destiny! God honors what our name means. John 10:3 says, "He calls His own sheep by name." This mean that He knows our name just like Shepherds name their sheep and count them each one by one. We are reminded in 2 Chronicles 7:14, that we are His people called by His name. It is up to us to make sure our names are written in the Lamb's Book of Life to live with Christ eternally. Jesus said whatever we ask our Father for in His Name, will be given!

When the Holy Spirit told Mary and Joseph that the baby she carried would be named Jesus, God was very specific in choosing that name. The Word makes it very clear to us that His Name is above every name;

> *"Therefore God exalted him to the highest place and gave him the name that is above every name, that at the name of Jesus every knee should bow, in heaven and on earth and under the earth,"*
> *Philippians 2:9-10 NIV*

we are to keep His name holy; everyone who calls on the name of Jesus will be saved; there is life and power in the name of Jesus! Healing comes, demons flee, the whole atmosphere changes when we speak the name of Jesus! His name is wonderful to me! I'm reminded of His power, His love, and His authority in me when I say the name Jesus!

Prayer:
Father, the name of Jesus is my greatest key to open doors to You and Your Kingdom! I ask first of all that You have my name written in the Lamb's Book of Eternal Life so that

I will spend eternity in Heaven with Jesus! Yes, this is my request! Then, I ask for a release of the Holy Spirit's power to empower me to be and do what I'm called for! Then I ask for a fresh release of grace, mercy and humility to realize that I am worthy to even call upon the name of the Lord! And it's all because of what Jesus died for on the Cross. Praise be To God for that name above all names! And to think that Jesus is now living in me! Is there anything I cannot do in His name? I call upon a fresh measure of faith to believe! The name of Jesus is greater than them all!
Amen

I declare the name of Jesus as the name above all names! His name is not only Lord, the Door, the Gate, but the key to unlock doors we will need to enter to demolish the power of the enemy to set captives free; doors to enter the promised-land we never knew existed. His name is greater than any obstruction, any enemy, any lie that comes against God's Kingdom. I command the powers of darkness to separate...God's power of light is overcoming all darkness!

ACTION STEPS:

✍ What does this mean to me?

✍ What must I do?

Order

Genesis chapter one says when God created the heavens and earth, He brought perfect order out of chaos. Everything was in total disarray, without form and empty. Darkness was hovering over the surface of the deep, and the Spirit of God was present to bring order. He spoke light into the heavens, waters of the sea, and earth to bring forth vegetation and life. He made evening and morning; he made the sun and the moon; the living creatures in the sea, and the birds of the air. He spoke to all of it saying, "Be fruitful and multiply each one after its own kind!" Everything God made, He said was very good (suitable and pleasant). He approved it completely.

In Chapter 2, He chose to create man in His own image by using the dust of the ground. He breathed the Spirit of Life into him and commanded him to rule and govern all that He had created. His work was to tend, guard and keep the Garden. God told him that he could eat freely of every tree in the Garden except for one - the Tree of the Knowledge of Good and Evil (or he would die).

God said, "Adam, it's not good for you to be alone, I will make a helper suitable, adapted, complementary for you!" So while Adam slept, God took one of his ribs and formed a woman. He brought her to help and assist Adam! It didn't take long for the Earth to get out of order again-anytime you take two opposing forces, especially a man and a woman, there's gonna be trouble!

Well, you know the rest of the story! Because Adam got the message from God about not eating from the forbidden tree, Eve got the word as well. When the serpent beguiled Eve and tempted her to partake, she believed the lie. "After all, did God really tell Adam that?" Sure enough, everything was in disarray, and darkness took over. Sin had entered the Garden and order, peace and abundant life were no more! Adam even got the idea that since he had all power and authority over everything in the Garden, he could also rule over Eve (uh, don't think so). God never gave Adam or Eve the power to rule and take authority over each other. His authority was to subdue the animals and the plants of the Garden. Adam and Eve were both given dual authority to rule, reign and bring order and peace. The Second Adam, Jesus, came along later to add Abundant Life!

So that my friend is a brief history of God's Creation over mankind and His desire for how to rule and reign together to build a new Kingdom on the Earth as it is in Heaven! In fact, it's called the Kingdom of Heaven and God planned all along for us to build His Kingdom here on the earth.

When God created Eve He told Adam He would give him a Helper. The biblical meaning of the word Helper is to cover, protect, aid, assist, surround and nurture. This whole idea God has of us becoming one flesh! Paul calls marriage a mystery! Never going to happen without the anointing of the Holy Spirit - and it still remains a miracle! But God said it was good! So, looks like it's up to you and me to make it good! We're supposed to get it together so we can teach our children what order in marriage and the home looks like. No wonder families are still so messed up!

When Jesus came on the scene years later, He came to finish what Adam was supposed to do! Build God's Kingdom on the Earth just like it was in Heaven. He came to earth as a man in humanity just like us! But

He left Earth fully in His Lordship! He came to set up His Kingdom with His Believers - those who would count the cost and do what He has called us to do! What if we totally fail? And when we look at the condition and moral decay present in our world today, it looks like we have totally failed. But let me give you another picture.

When you are tuned in to the prophetic, the Kingdom News that is being lived, declared, and fought for in this generation...it is incredible! When I see what God is doing just right here in Tulsa, Oklahoma, I am amazed! I'm aware of families, homes, churches, home groups, students, camps, and homeless shelters, gang bangers who are turning lives around and building His Kingdom in their own mountains (education, church, home, business, family, government, and entertainment). And when you look at how out of order those mountains have become, it truly is a miracle that God is raising up warriors to take those mountains today for His Kingdom! We are seeking and finding the Kingdom and when we don't find it, we start building it wherever we are!

Let's give Him permission to bring order to our chaos, our homes and families, our places of influence...and just watch how things change! Don't wait for things and our leaders to bring change. You have power and authority to make it happen! Your Position has been

> *"But [we are different, because] our citizenship is in heaven. And from there we eagerly await [the coming of] the Savior, the Lord Jesus Christ; who, by exerting that power which enables Him even to subject everything to Himself, will [not only] transform [but completely refashion] our earthly bodies so that they will be like His glorious resurrected body."*
> *Philippians 3:20-21 AMP*

elevated to the palace! Even as Esther was called to save the Jews and was willing to perish in the process. You are called to influence those who have the power to bring order out of chaos. Humble yourself and get God's heart on how to do it! God's Servants become those who govern!

Prayer:
Father, we repent for Adam's sin which has become our sin. We are called to bring order out of chaos that is loosed in our world, but we must admit that we are just as guilty of not bringing forth order, peace, righteousness and joy. We don't always desire to put right what is out of order. Our hearts, homes and families all cry out for order and yet we choose to live in the chaos without electing to bring forth change. Father, forgive us when we compromise and settle for the mess. Release the passion within us to desire order and set out to bring that order now! Give us desire, strength, passion and even people to help. We were not meant to live in chaos and clutter, so grant us courage Lord; supply a bountiful supply of courage to arise to end clutter and chaos. You are a God of order. All the universe must remain in position to obey what You created it for. Help us to desire that same order and blessing in our lives and declare war on disorder.
In Jesus' name
Amen

I declare righteousness, peace and joy over my life, my home, my meetings, my heart. I can bring this order when I command the blessing and promise of Jesus. He has given me power and authority to rule over all chaos and darkness. Disorder is not from God...His plan is for order, peace, agreement, no discord! When opinions differ (and they will), agreement (choosing to agree in disagreement) must rule. Otherwise strife and argument will arise. Offense/defense must not be allowed to divide; separate. Unity must be attained. Agreement goes beyond opinion!

ACTION STEPS:

✍ What does this mean to me?

✍ What must I do?

Purpose

To fulfill this scripture by living in harmony and being of the same mind, takes a willingness and a miracle! When we get an understanding of our purpose, and we find the position where we can use our gifting to the fullest, we find great joy!

Without a vision, people are confused, and without focus or goals. Training your people to carry your vision, and your mission statement can make all the difference. Many times as I listen to people share, they are simply going through the motions of the day, but are without real goal or purpose. We are promised a life of abundance, but many settle for a hum-drum, same old existence with no joy or delight in it.

I learned a valuable lesson years ago of the importance of a mission statement! It helps you discover and determine your own strengths, desires, and weaknesses, and gives a new direction for where to place your time and gifting. It totally changes what you have to do, to what you absolutely love doing! It helps you discern how you can best use your gifts in helping and leading others. Your

> "...make my joy complete by being of the same mind, having the same love [toward one another], knit together in spirit, intent on one purpose [and living a life that reflects your faith and spreads the gospel—the good news regarding salvation through faith in Christ]."
> Philippians 2:2 AMP

dream can become your life's work! It changes what you dread and dislike doing, into a challenge and delight as you go to work each day. Design, work out, organize, teach, and find out what you are really good at doing! This is amazing! It's what gets you up in the morning with excitement and joy wondering what you will create today! Every family, business, church needs to know and understand the purpose for their existence. Do your employees know the purpose of your business or your mission to accomplish? What makes your church unique? Or your family? There are many Christian churches meeting all over the world. What is the main mission of your church and how does your purpose fit into its outreach? What you stand for as a church, business, or even a family should be posted and imparted to everyone. It is your identity. Without a vision, mission, or purpose, people wander aimlessly.

When I was able to take tests to help determine what my giftings were, then it could direct me into the areas I could thrive in. I failed at too many things in the process because I just didn't fit and considered myself a failure! Oh what a difference it made when I discovered there were certain things I could do well and loved doing them. You can see how easily this happens when you don't know who you are, have no real identity, and are easily swayed by public opinion. God has a purpose and a plan for our future. Before you and I were born, He anointed us for a specific task on earth, a mission for us to accomplish, and then He sent us forth to seek, find and accomplish it. You will know it when you find it! And as you grow in it, be ready for it to change you, and take you higher in your development. You keep loving it knowing you are right in the purpose that God has purposed for you! Read Jeremiah 1:5! Consider these quotes that have left a great impression on my life for many years:

> *"The greatest tragedy in life is not death, but living life without purpose!"*
>
> *"The greatest frustration in life is being in a job or task that you are successful in, but you really don't like what you do!"*
>
> *-Myles Monroe*

Time to re-calculate, re-think and re-evaluate! Ask the Lord what he has in mind for you today and don't expect it to be something that you dislike! He desires for you to find your calling! He's the One who planted it in you!

Most everyone wants to help others, but how? Here are some great questions to possibly help! What do you absolutely love doing? It could be a hobby, building things, fixing things, creating, finding better ways of doing business or helping people? It could be the question why somebody doesn't invent a...? I wanted to help others learn what I was learning! You, too, can find a need and fill it-especially if you love doing it! Or, who is doing something today that you wish you were doing?

Clarity and understanding of the purpose for your life is an ongoing quest! Your search for a meaningful life and one that makes a difference should motivate you to keep on asking the Lord what His purpose is for you today, and the days to come. How can I best serve You Lord?

Life is way too short to spend every day disliking what you are doing for hours at a time. Each delighted employee, happy family member, or boss simply found a greater way to do what he/she does, or found a better way to use his/her skills. Maybe you carry the very idea, better way, or suggestion. Your purpose awaits! Identify who you are and what you stand for!

> "Then the Lord answered me and said, "Write the vision and engrave it plainly on [clay] tablets so that the one who reads it will run. For the vision is yet for the appointed [future] time. It hurries toward the goal [of fulfillment]; it will not fail. Even though it delays, wait [patiently] for it, because it will certainly come; it will not delay."
> Habakkuk 2:2-3 AMP

Work with your family to help them discover and know the family mission and what you want to accomplish as a family. Install the importance of honoring the family name. Make a sign and have it hanging in your home for all to see! Perhaps it could read like one of these others have written:

"Outdo one another in showing love!"

"Making a difference is our goal!"

"Purpose and destiny is our mission!"

"We grow people!"

"We know the way, come join us!"

This is why we can be in full accord and harmonious with one another, we're not vying for the same position! We know our purpose and can't wait to fulfill it! It's the Kingdom way!

My personal mission statement is to lead, encourage, and ignite passion in others to love and serve God by discovering and fulfilling their purpose for God's Kingdom on earth.

Prayer:
Father, before I was ever born, I believe You had a specific purpose and destiny for me to fulfill here on earth. My highest desire is to fulfill this call. Help me to not only seek my calling, but to find it! I want to be all you created me to be and do. I also know when I please You, I will know Your favor and delight. Holy Spirit, I ask You to open doors for me to know fully how to serve the Lord to my highest and most excellent way. Help my joy be totally full to overflowing when I discover it.
Amen

I declare purpose to begin to float to the surface as folks read this book. Clarity and direction to those uncertain. If we don't have a vision, purpose, direction then we are stopped. But with a purpose, we excel and move forward. It's a day of rising up and moving forward. God desires for you to be certain who you are and your purpose in this season. May you be fully persuaded to know and step into your purpose/destiny!

ACTION STEPS:

✍ What does this mean to me?

✍ What must I do?

Quietness

> *"For the Lord God, the Holy One of Israel has said this,*
> *"In returning [to me] and rest you shall be saved,*
> *In quietness and confident trust is your strength."*
> *Isaiah 30:15 AMP*

Don't those words just feel like warm oil pouring forth all over you? Are you hearing our Shepherd calling you from a verse in Song of Solomon saying, Rise up, my fair one, and come away with Me? Come away with me My promised Bride. You have ravished My heart! Do your hear yourself responding, "I am my Beloved's, and His desire is towards me!"

This is my quest for the day. I long for His strength, and I find it in my quiet moments alone with Him. We live in a very loud, invasive atmosphere today. Quietness must be sought after, and we have to find the quiet button! Constant noise brings chaotic thinking and our souls are longing for the stillness that only comes when we choose it. That may mean a walk in the woods, a ride alone in the car, or finding a peaceful spot to listen to the birds. Choose to close the door to others and rest in His presence!

Quietness means undisturbed, peaceful, turning off all noise, listening to a waterfall, or beautiful music to quiet your soul. To see Jesus as your Shepherd, the lover of your soul! To know His love over you will replenish your heart. Allow Him to speak and convince you that there is a plan and future waiting for you. Know and totally believe that He exists, He knows your name, and His plans for you are good and purposeful. Oh how He loves you and longs to have your attention.

Turn off all the loudness and noise, and run away to be in His Presence to find quietness and strength. His invitation is always yes and amen! His requesting of your presence is constant, and you must draw near in this present day!

Yada means to know (biblically), intimately by uniting and coming together as one! To Yada the Lord is likened to becoming one in marriage - the only one you choose to be intimate with. This is the time you choose

> *"Come and let us return [in repentance] to the Lord, for He has torn us, but He will heal us; He has wounded us, but He will bandage us."* *"So let us know and become personally acquainted with Him; let us press on to know and understand fully the [greatness of the] Lord [to honor, heed, and deeply cherish Him]. His appearing is prepared and is as certain as the dawn, and He will come to us [in salvation] like the [heavy] rain, like the spring rain watering the earth."* Hosea 6:1, 3

to come away to hear His voice; to feel His touch; to sense His favor, and His kisses. Confirm and seal your love for Him and receive your daily quietness and strength!

Prayer:
Jesus, what a wonder you are! You have chosen me as your Bride! You are my bright Morningstar, my soon-coming King, and my Bridegroom; the One who never leaves me but has promised to be my constant companion. Your lovingkindness is better than life! Thank You my Lord, my Savior, my All in All! You have truly captured my heart. I gladly will follow you all the days of my life! Thank You! Amen

---

I declare peace, stillness, rest, quietness over your soul today. It you are felling pressures, stress, chaos, then agree with me that no weapon formed against you will prosper! You choose peace, order, quietness for your soul! Don't settle for the lies and accusing of the enemy. He puts up a smoke screen to bring chaos and doubt. Command the blessing of peace! Don't tolerate, argue, or put up with it...it's not from God!

ACTION STEPS:

✎ What does this mean to me?

✎ What must I do?

Reflect and Radiate

To reflect means to emanate, match, take after, resonate, copy, follow, imitate, reproduce, and return. Radiance is defined as brightness, brilliant, sparkle, light, shooting forth in all directions, glowing.

Who among us would not want to believe that we Believers all carry the glory

> *"And we all, who with unveiled faces contemplate the Lord's glory, are being transformed into his image with ever-increasing glory, which comes from the Lord, who is the Spirit."*
> *2 Corinthians 3:18 NIV*

and majesty of our Lord Jesus Christ? The Word says He lives in me and He is greater in me than me!

Amazing! If that be true, then we have to believe the above scriptures that simply prove this to be true.

Are you experiencing the transforming power and glory of His transforming in you? Are you noticing the old things that once were part of you, are no longer? Anger, blame, strong judgement of others, use of bad language, and self-will? According to the Word, if we truly believe that He is in us, then we are as He is on the earth. I reflect His Glory by being like Him, imitating and reproducing Him, and abounding in the fruits of the

> *"The Son is the radiance of God's glory and the exact representation of his being, sustaining all things by his powerful word. After he had provided purification for sins, he sat down at the right hand of the Majesty in heaven." Hebrews 1:3 NIV*

Spirit. We are doing what He would do by being, fellowshipping, and loving people...people of all color, races, beliefs and those who don't yet know Jesus! No judgment, no prejudice, no blame!

We carry His radiance which is His glory! We walk in the supernatural and should be trusting Him to bring forth His miracles of healing and deliverance used to set people free from darkness and disease. Jesus came to dispel the darkness and destroy the works of the devil! I am not seeing near enough of His glory in me to do these things. How about you?

Another "R" word that we use to describe ourselves is religious! That's where I fall short. I walked too many years in religion, and not in the radiance of His miracle working power! Since being filled with His Spirit, my life is abounding with His image, glory and radiance.

Will you join me in confessing and repenting before the Lord that we are more concerned about how people see us instead of being concerned about reflecting his radiance, the fullness of His glory, and His miracle-working power? His Kingdom was lived before us as Jesus went about doing good. This is the hour; this is the day He has made for change, and He reminds us to do what He did. If our hearts are truly filled with His radiance and reflection, this should be effortless! He lives greater in me than me!

> Prayer:
> Lord, I give You permission to turn up the lights! Turn on the power in me to shine, Jesus shine! Let my eyes so see the need in others to be greater than my own. I desire the aura of Your Presence and the brightness of Your light within to go before me and light the way for others! Illuminate me to walk thru the darkness of this world. Father, because of You, we can all shine with Your glory, and reflect Your radiance on the earth as it is in Heaven! This is almost too much for us to comprehend, and we settle for our own understanding instead. Forgive our unbelief and surprise us with Your brilliance which is living on the inside of we who believe. Help us release the power to be all that You are within us! What a wonder You are!
> In Jesus' name
> Amen

We all need R & R...reflecting and radiance!! I believe the old saying is true, "You become like who you spend time with!" Perhaps more time spent with Jesus is the key, you think?

I declare this day, that you and I are direct reflections of our Lord Jesus Christ. He lives greater in you and I. We are to extol His greatness, His love! And His radiant presence within in us is fully able to reflect His glory within. Repent right now of any ill-will, separation, anger, self-righteousness that would prevent His divine reflection from shining through you. Let the Greater One within shine!

ACTION STEPS:

✍ What does this mean to me?

✍ What must I do?

Smile

Proverbs 31 is all about the virtuous woman and how ambitious and strong she is in the Lord. She is used as an example for how all women can become. Verse 10 says she is capable, intelligent, and virtuous, and she is more precious than jewels. Her value is far about rubies or pearls! She is a good manager, know how to be successful in business, and is a good manager

> *"Strength and dignity are her clothing and her position is strong and secure; and she smiles at the future [knowing that she and her family are prepared]."*
> *Proverbs 31:25 AMP*

of her household. She's an organizer, a gardener, and she conditions her body, mind and spirit. She knows how to handle stress and refuses to gossip, be discontent, or be filled with self-pity. She reverently and worshipfully fears the Lord. Many praise her! Even her children rise up and call her blessed; her husband boasts and praises her by saying, "You excel them all!"

I have experienced some rather extreme health issues over the past six months and was given some reports that I didn't want to hear. Suddenly my "normal" for living changed from being a rather easy, laid-back existence to a more radical, scheduled day where the taking of meds, exercise, and doctor appointments became necessary for life itself. In other words, it was ordered by four doctors, a physical therapist, and a chiropractor to lower my salt intake, exercise and rest. All of this was a result of a stroke and heart issues. When you "code blue" and recover, you realize your life is not your own. God must be in charge! The sweetest words I remember hearing were, "We've got a pulse!"

I have walked my life, for the most part, as an ambitious woman – strong in the Lord and the power of His might. Suddenly, my strength and future began to depend on medication and exercise with limitations of strength and balance often wondering if I did everything I was supposed to do that day. Sometimes yes; sometimes no! Still I trust the Lord that His plans for me were for good. I kept

> *"Beat your plowshares into swords and your pruning hooks into spears; Let the weak say, "I am strong!"*
> *Joel 3:10 AMP*

hearing inside from the Holy Spirit, "My plans for you are to fulfill the destiny you were born for. Arise and go forth! Smile at the future!" I even received a great sign from my son Mike that says, "She smiles at the future."

So my word for the "S" in the alphabet today is smile. I'm sure you have read the importance of what happens in your body when you smile. It changes the endorphins, the way you think, the atmosphere around you, and it's contagious to others. So, I smile...not just because I was raised up to live and not die, but because God has plans and a purpose for me and has graced me with more days to

> *"He will yet fill your mouth with laughter and your lips with shouts of joy."*
> *Job 8:21 NIV*

fulfill those plans. We can smile because we are in readiness for the future. We have planned for it, arranged for it, and made necessary provision for it-not only for ourselves, but for our families as well. This is a picture of a virtuous, happy, prepared woman. She teaches, trains, tells, and loves her family enough to leave them skilled and secure for the future. They too can live smiling at the future knowing Jesus Christ is Lord. He has written their names in His book of life when they choose to love the Lord with all their heart, mind, and spirit. They know their future is a good one!

Living forever in God's Kingdom with Jesus...that should make you smile. We know who holds our future now and forevermore! Smiles are contagious! Next time

you go to the grocery story, walk in with a big smile and

watch how others respond.

Prayer:
Father, help me to choose happy! To choose everyday to
say, "I think I'll just be happy today!" Help us to smile in
the midst of tragedy and trauma. We are seeing great
distress today with the hurricanes bringing destruction;
people helpless in the storms and having to leave their
homes. Yet, we smile knowing God specializes in bringing
beauty from ashes.
Amen

> I declare and have decided, "I will smile at the future!" I have prepared my household to love Jesus, serve Him, lay down their lives for Him and trust each of them to make wise decisions. I trust the Lord to guide me, protect me and comfort me all my days on earth. Then, to lift me to live forever with Him. Now that's what'll make me smile.

ACTION STEPS:

✍ What does this mean to me?

✍ What must I do?

Triumph, Triumphed

Moses and the Israelites sang this song to the Lord:

> "...I will sing to the Lord, for He has triumphed gloriously; the horse and its rider He has thrown into the sea."
> Exodus 15:1 AMP

So, what does this say to you? Perhaps singing a triumphant song to the Lord is a great idea? Can you imagine the fear and dread when the Israelites were standing on the shores of the Red Sea and started in on

Moses, "Did you bring us out here to die?" Remember how God spoke to Moses,

> *"...Do not be afraid! Take your stand [be firm and confident and undismayed] and see the salvation of the Lord which He will accomplish for you today; for those Egyptians whom you have seen today, you will never see again. The Lord will fight for you while you [only need to] keep silent and remain calm."*
> *Exodus 14:13-14 AMP*

What a dilemma! They had to trust in the Lord, and trust in Moses, to deliver them from the Egyptians and get them across that Red Sea! Well, you know the rest of the story! The Israelites walked across the sea on dry land as the waters parted. The Lord saved Israel and they saw the Egyptians washed up dead on the seashore. The people fervently

> *"Then Miriam the Prophetess and sister of Aaron, took a tambourine in hand, and all the women went out after her with timbrels and dancing! "Sing to the Lord, for He has triumphed gloriously and is highly exalted; the horse and his rider He has thrown into the sea."*
> *Exodus 15:20-21 AMP*

feared the Lord and trusted in (relied on, remained steadfast to) the Lord and His Servant Moses.

The Lord was faithful with His Word and Moses was faithful to trust the Lord to do what He said He would do! Isn't that the leadership we look for today? Leaders who are willing to hear and trust the

"O my God, in You I [have unwavering] trust [and I rely on You with steadfast confidence], Do not let me be ashamed or my hope in You be disappointed; Do not let my enemies triumph over me."
Psalms 25:2 AMP

Word of the Lord and dare to step out and follow His lead. I truly believe that is the kind of faith-filled leader

"But thanks be to God, who always leads us in triumph in Christ, and through us spreads and makes evident everywhere the sweet fragrance of the knowledge of Him."
2 Corinthians 2:14 AMP

we need to follow in this day. Those we can trust to follow through with the test to reach the triumph...who won't bail out in the middle of the sea! The real test is to finish what God has spoken. Don't Quit! Have obedient hearts to hear, follow, and stand fast until we triumph! And don't forget to sing the song of triumph! It'll make you smile and triumph gloriously! It's one thing to be the follower, and another to be the leader! Choose this day which you are willing to be!

Prayer:
Father, we long to hear Your voice as we travel the path with You! We must learn to listen, and be quick to obey no matter how preposterous or presumptuous it sounds! You look for those who would dare to step out full-knowing they are getting ready to triumph! That would be us! So we ask for Your gift of faith to be released in each of us this day. We not only want to hear, but turn to the people and say, "Follow me, I know the way!" And when the people say to you, "Did you bring us here to die?" Your answer is No! Not if you have heard the voice of the Lord! Remember what you have said "yes" to. It's that faith and determination that gets Christ's attention. Warriors, soldiers, the Army of the Lord who stay the course. Never give up! Do I get a witness? If so, say Amen!

I declare over every situation in my life…the devil is defeated and has no control over my life or future! Jesus causes me to triumph and I will not fail! It is written! That is my stand and I won't back down.

ACTION STEPS:

✍ What does this mean to me?

✍ What must I do?

Unite, Unity

To unite means to *join, meet, merge, band together, become one, entwine, pull together, join forces, fuse, wed, partner together.*

How many Christians today cannot even agree on this! Did Jehovah God create the heavens and the earth? Have you been in a meeting lately where all those present lifted their voices together with one united mind to God?

> *"The Apostles lifted their voices together with one united mind to God and said, O Sovereign Lord, You are He who made the Heaven and the Earth, the Sea and everything that is in them."*
> *Acts 4:24 AMP*

125

To agree is *to be in unison; of the same opinion; harmonious; one accord; minds in full agreement.* I believe that God just loves it when His kids walk together in unity and agreement. Does that mean we are all totally thinking alike in how we see things, or how we would go about doing what needs to be done? Of course not! However, we are all united in one Lord, one purpose, one baptism, and one mission....to bring the Kingdom to the earth as it

> *"But I urge you brethren, by the name of our Lord Jesus Christ, that all of you be in perfect harmony and full agreement in what you say, and that there be no dissensions or factions or divisions among you, but that you be perfectly united in your common understanding and in your opinions and judgements." "I know there are factions, contentions and wrangling among some of the households! This should not be so!"*
> *I Corinthians 1:10-11 AMP*

is in Heaven! We can all agree and unite in that outreach! Lord knows we are all going to go about doing that in a totally different way! The way we each walk our walk and hear His voice is totally different. We all are seeking to walk in different pathways, yet knowing

126

there is ONE WAY! As we discover our different ways of using the gifts God has given us, as well as our different personalities, our ways of ministry are going to vary...and that's alright. The purpose is the same, the goal is the same! The outcome should be that we all come to the saving grace of Jesus and we do this in harmony making beautiful music. This takes some maturity in learning how to live together, be in ministry together, and giving each other freedom to function. No

> *"Again I tell you, if two of you on earth agree (harmonize together, make a symphony together) about anything and everything they may ask, it will come to pass and be done for them by My Father in Heaven. For where two or three are gathered (drawn together as My Followers in My Name, there I Am in the midst of them." Matthew 18:19-20 AMP*

competition, no superiority, no judgement, but total freedom! Some say this takes a miracle!

Some excel in leading others to Christ; others excel in discipling and raising up strong leaders; others love to help others to intercede with passion and fervency! A missing link in the church has been developing the gifts of prophecy, prayer for miracles, supernatural gifts, and healings. We must hear the voice of the Lord for this generation!

Faith is something we are all longing for, and yet look how divided we are in the Body of Christ about what that looks like. God loves to lavish us with supernatural power so that we will go beyond our own understanding! When we judge one another and the way we minister, we find ourselves out of sync and out of agreement with God's will! Even the Apostles and Disciples had some disagreements about the way ministry should be done. Sometimes they parted ways to be more effective and in agreement with each other. Learn not to criticize, judge, or gossip, but rejoice in the various ways God can release His power! God desires freedom, healing, setting captives free, and followers! Are you doing your part and what you are destined for? The one you are responsible for is you! That is unless you are a parent, pastor, discipler, mentor, shepherd, or one who has a heart to bring unity and agreement among the brothers and sisters.

People are supposed to see how sweet it is to dwell together in unity! Let's challenge ourselves to be that one who chooses to walk in peace and be a peacemaker! We are not just to make converts, but raise up DOERS of the Word - disciples! We should be fruitful in raising up and multiplying the Kingdom with functioning, powerful, Spirit filled disciples and trained leaders to release the power and glory of Jesus! The greatest way the early Believers were recognized, was by their love!

> *"All of the Disciples with their minds in full agreement and unity, devoted themselves steadfastly to prayer, waiting together with the women, Mary and Jesus' brothers."*
> *Acts 1:14 AMP*

Now that is where we must agree and unite! That's how we should be known. Let's choose to be the true Believers of today so that others will say, "Wow, look at those Christians, how they love!" And this is how this works! In every part of society, if you are a Believer in Jesus, you should show forth love in your family, in your marriage, in your business, in your daily living, in your church, in the school, in the board meeting, on the streets, out in public, with other Believers, at the party, in the neighborhood, at the restaurant, at the grocery, in the drive-thru, in the movies, in the mall, and above all parents....let your love be over-abundant with your children. You are the greatest influence for your children no matter how they feel about their peers! In every area of culture today, unity is lacking! What would happen in the political, governmental arena if unity and agreement was released? Our nation would become great again, that's what! If we get behind our representatives, senators, and especially our President...oh my, this is what will cause God to bless America once again! UNITY - UNITED - UNITE ="U" and this definitely means you!

This letter of the alphabet can be the greatest challenge of all. Remember what Jesus said in Matthew 18:20, "Where two or three are gathered, there's gonna be trouble," (or something like that). Set your mind and heart right now on how you will handle conflict and difference of opinion! Regardless of the American way, you are not #1, nor do you need to control the world. Give it up! Humble yourself to take a step back. You are on a different track than the fast track. You are after agreement, unity, oneness, and becoming one with the Lord Jesus Christ! Nobody loses on His team. Read the back of the book and you'll see that WE WIN!! WARNING: this will cost you your way! Have fun with this!

There is only one way for this to happen...choose to live for Christ. Do what He did; live like He lived; serve like He served; and be willing to die like He died! Choose a life of unity, agreement, and favor with God and man. It's the only way to be happy in Jesus and to stand in His favor and Sonship!! Feel His pleasure and

delight as you choose life! Don't expect this to make you

popular.

> Prayer:
> Father, unity is impossible without the power of the Holy
> Spirit released in each of us! Would You fill us afresh NOW
> with Your Spirit to not only enable us, but empower us to
> be fused, connected, united, join forces with, become one
> with, and fully choose to embrace Your life within us! That
> only happens when we give You permission! We do that
> NOW! I repent Lord for the negative spirit I war against
> within me. Forgive me when I have such aught against
> others. I repent and long for Your Sweet Holy Spirit to
> change my heart Oh God, make me ever new! Change my
> heart oh Lord-make me more like You!
> Amen

I declare to choose unity! I want to make beautiful music together,
words God can use! Harmonize in unity! I refuse disunity,
disagreement! I cannot accept it...I believe in Christ, we lift our
voices together in unity, harmony, making a beautiful symphony.
That's what I'm after!

ACTION STEPS:

✍ What does this mean to me?

✍ What must I do?

Virtuous

Virtue means moral excellence, ideal, upright, ethical conduct, a good thing, honorable, honest, merit, fineness, excellent character, generous, kind, innocent, faithful, temperate, faithful, hopeful, chaste, great worth, love is greater than fear, hard worker, prudent, successful in business, strong, extends arms to the poor, industrious, strong and dignified, loves to laugh (especially at the future), not easily offended, wise, manager of her household, has great reward from her husband, one who honors and fears the Lord. She makes her husband proud. She is well-known for her virtuous deeds. She is one good woman!

Guys, if you are looking for a wife, this is a good list to work from! Girls, if you are wanting to check your qualifications as a virtuous wife, or a courageous "wanna-be," then this is a good list to follow. We girls must remember we didn't have proper training to be this virtuous woman. Most of us have had to learn as we go, or had to find out the hard way what in the world a virtuous wife would possibly look like, right? And this

> *"An excellent woman [one who is spiritual, capable, intelligent, and virtuous], who is he who can find her? Her value is more precious than jewels and her worth is far above rubies or pearls!"* Proverbs 31:10 AMP

current generation has not even heard the word...v i r t u o u s!! Don't go looking for a virtuous woman in the crowd! She is a picture of what God sees as a woman who fears the Lord! One who would make an excellent wife!! Sure doesn't fit the role model of today, does it?

If you are a woman looking for an opportunity to teach and train women how to be virtuous, then step right up and let your requests be made known. Not a small task!

Women of today don't have many role models who can train in business expertise or how to function as a woman in the marketplace, home, or even in the church. Gain understanding of who you are, and God's plan and purpose for your life. Know that His plans are to prosper you and fill you with wisdom and knowledge to elevate you to the higher level. Your attitude will determine your altitude of thinking. It is time to think beyond the norm and choose to walk in excellence, virtue, and honor. You are unique and God has your destiny waiting just for you! Remember, you've gotta go low to go high.

Now, before you go thinking I'm searching for the total woman, think again...unless you are a religious church lady! For many years, women tried to look right, act right, wear the right righteous robes, and look every bit the part of a God-fearing woman, but our hearts were filled with selfishness, self-will, and judgement of those who didn't look the part! Thank God we are delivered from that stinkin' thinkin'! The more we learn to love Jesus with all of our hearts, everything in us will desire to please Him and simply do what He did while on earth. A virtuous woman is one who has learned the purpose of her life and chooses to walk in her full identity. She's happy with who God created her to be, and she celebrates it with all her heart. She delights in pleasing the Lord by dying to selfish ways and choosing to fall in love with the Lord daily! Her only desire is to please Him. All of the fruits and results of a redeemed heart are hers, and she worships and praises the one true God with all of her heart.

Remember, God doesn't look at your past, your accomplishments, your mistakes, or even your wrong choices! He sees a heart that delights in lifting standards of living to prove to the world, that to live for

Christ, is the only way to attain the reward of a virtuous woman. Look over that list of virtues again. It must be possible or the Lord would not have given us these choices. A woman who carries these qualities should be in great demand...not just for a husband, but in every part of society/culture. Rare indeed! What a blessing to find a group of women who long to live this rare lifestyle and who choose to study what living in the Kingdom looks like! The Holy Spirit will empower us to practice together and find great delight in the eyes of the Lord! After all, our Bridegroom is the one to please. Choose this day who and how you will serve...the world's way or the Kingdom Way! Keep searching for a team who truly desires Jesus to be the Lord of their life.

Prayer:
Father, Jesus came to the earth to reveal and expose His Kingdom on the earth as it is in Heaven! We are still grasping to understand how we can live this Kingdom life. We know it is a choice, but we also know we have learned the ways of the world all too well. The Kingdom way is a total renewal of the mind and allows our minds to be transformed by Your Spirit. Lord, renew us to be Your virtuous women who have chosen your way as the only

way and who long to be changed into Your image!
Amen

I declare virtue over every woman reading this. Your value, your beauty, your influence is far more precious that the finest jewels. You have great moral excellence, conduct. I challenge you to say "I am generous, kind, faithful, temperate, hopeful, chaste, holy, of great worth, filled with perfect love with no fear for the future. I'm strong, successful in business, I extend my hands to the poor, I love to laugh, not easily offended, wise, manager of my household, I honor and fear the Lord. I don't strive for perfection but purity of heart.

ACTION STEPS:

✍ What does this mean to me?

✍ What must I do?

Wonderful Wonder Women

Oh Jesus, what a wonder You are! The awe and wonder of your glory and brilliance is greater than the brightest star! It's greater than the magnificent heavens on a starlit night! Your wonderful light that has called us out of the darkness. Your statutes,

> "Praise be to the Lord, for he showed me the wonders of His love when I was in a city under siege."
> Psalms 31:21 NIV

knowledge and love are far too wonderful for me to grasp! You have shown me the wonder of your great love! Open my eyes that I may see wonderful things in

Your law. Even Your knowledge is too wonderful for me, too lofty for me to attain. Let me understand Your precepts; then I will meditate on your wonders! You have promised to show wonders in the heavens and on the earth. All of those wonderful words taken from the Old Testament.

Then Peter repeats what Joel said in Acts 2:22:

> *"In the last days, God says, I will pour out my Spirit on all people. Your sons and daughters will prophesy, your young men will see visions, your old men will dream dreams. Even on my servants, both men and women, I will pour out my Spirit in those days, and they will prophesy. I will show wonders in the heavens above and signs on the earth below, blood and fire and billows of smoke. The sun will be turned to darkness and the moon to blood before the coming of the great and glorious day of the Lord. And everyone who calls on the name of the Lord will be saved."*
> *Acts 2:17-21 NIV*

Jesus of Nazareth was a man accredited by God to you by miracles, signs, and wonders, which God did through Him, as you know!" As a result of this mighty sermon by Peter at Pentecost, and when the people heard, they were cut to the heart and said, "What must we do?" Peter replied, "Repent and be baptized every one of you, in the name of Jesus Christ for the forgiveness of your sins. And they received the gift of the Holy Spirit. For this is the promise for you and your children and for all those who are far off (us today)...for all the Lord our God will call." This includes everyone – young and old, all races, cultures, males and females, Protestants and Catholics, denominations and charismatics.

So my question to you is: Have you received the Gift of the Holy Spirit Baptism which will empower you to do the wonderful works that Jesus did? If not, then you are not fully equipped for battle and are limited only by what you know in your understanding. But with His power and by His Spirit, we can begin to see and experience his wonder, awe, glory, supernatural and wonderful words of life come to pass on the earth as it is in Heaven! And remember He spoke that our children and every Believer we meet, needs to receive His power and glory! When is the last time you prayed for someone to receive His power and might? Today is the day of signs, wonders, and miracles! Let's do this!

As we meet together in the name of the Lord, we need the power that we receive from one another. Expect miracles when we gather; expect the Wonder of Wonders to show up and wow us with His love power and awe! When we expect to see His wonder, it gives Him the permission to release all that we ask for! And even more!

Prayer:
Father, You have a wonderful plan for your family to thrive and excel. You sent Jesus to show us, Your Word to reveal to us; Your Holy Spirit to teach us, and each other to encourage us to show forth Your wonderful works and words in action! Forgive us when we tend to only walk by our own understanding and according to our own comfort. We want Your wonder and Your power, and yet we forget to EXPECT! Would you please bring forth Your wonder and remind us it is Your Glory we seek and it is not up to our ability and works! But by Your Spirit and Power! May we receive a fresh Pentecost to go forth and bring wonder to a sleepy church and a dark world! Bring it forth in me, Lord! I choose to hear and obey!
Amen

Because I am filled with the Holy Spirit power of Almighty God, I declare His wonder working power at work in me! I have the same power to heal, raise the dead, case out demons and depression. If Jesus lives in me (and He does), that same power exists today in all believers in Jesus who choose to believe. I can do all things through Christ because of His wonder-working power, His wonderful words of life! And because God chose a woman to birth the Son of God 2000 years ago, why wouldn't He still use woman to birth His purpose on the earth today? I stand ready to serve you Lord Jesus today as a woman of wonder, what would please my King? How can I change a family, a nation today for Your glory? Here I am Lord, send me! I declare it this day! In Jesus' name.

ACTION STEPS:

✐ What does this mean to me?

✐ What must I do?

Xerxes

There once was a king named Xerxes who ruled and reigned over his royal throne from the citadel of Susa. God used a young girl named Esther to win his favor, and save her people the Jews! She became his Queen and humbly won his approval over all the other young virgins. She stayed humble before him and would constantly say to him, "If it please the king," and then offer her suggestion. She knew her role and influence over the king was to change his mind and spare her people. She said to him in Esther 7:3, "If I have found favor with you, Your Majesty, and if it pleases you, grant me my life—this is my petition. And spare my people—this is my request." (NIV)

You probably know the rest of the story, Haman was set to destroy the Jews and Esther knew she had the power and influence to turn the heart of the King. She remained humble and would keep her words filled with requests to the King. Her humility and desire to please the King kept her in his favor and he granted her request. We celebrate Purim to this day because of Esther's obedience and courage! She was willing to die to save her people! "If I perish, I perish," she quoted. She knew she was born for that time and season, and God gave her favor to become Queen and influence Favor with the King!

Men have power, but women have influence! As women, we must have the mind of Christ to function by His Spirit. Otherwise, we become like the world's system and cry out, "I am Woman, hear me Roar!" We roar for our rights, our equality, our way, and even our wills to rule! How things change for we women, when our attitude changes and we say, like Esther, "If it please the King, or my Boss, or my husband, or God's Will over mine!" It's not about who wins, but staying faithful, pleasing our King! Not my will, but Thine, Oh Lord!

Call it submission, or a willing heart, God loves it when we honor one another. This is not a male / female issue; this is submitting to a Father's Love and trusting Him to bring order and success. We come into order by hearing His voice and honoring His way of honoring one another! Come on women, we don't need the reputation of a powerful lady! As we honor God in humility and assurance, God will bring forth His desire. Someone said that we women are power in a velvet glove! We don't have to prove how strong we are, our identity and inner knowing, is our strength! All the more reason to know who you are and know that God's purpose and destiny is being fulfilled in your life! That is truly fulfillment for us women!

For Esther, her mission statement could have read: "My mission is to save my people, the Jews!" Just that simple! It was not just to marry the King - that was the vehicle God used to reach the heart of the King. So, we women carry great influence for the Kingdom! Let's lay down our need to prove our strength, our purpose, our success, and ask God to reveal His purpose and destiny for our lives as He designed us. That's where our true contentment and favor excels! Esther knew she was Mordecai's niece, but also her greater identity was she was born to become Queen and save her people the Jews!

> *"Arise, shine, for your light has come, and the glory of the Lord rises upon you. See, darkness covers the earth and thick darkness is over the peoples, but the Lord rises upon you and his glory appears over you. Nations will come to your light, and kings to the brightness of your dawn."*
> *Isaiah 60:1-3 NIV*

Are you in the position you are called to? Are you fulfilling the call of God for why you were born? If God could use a powerful person like King Xerxes, to fulfill His purpose, and chose a little peasant girl named Esther to send to the Palace, why couldn't He use you and me to bring forth His purpose on earth today? Let's arise to the High Calling God anointed us for before we were born, and be ready and willing to live as Esther..."for such a time as this!"

Prayer:
Father, only You know my frame, heart, destiny and position. You are my designer/creator and know where I can best be suited to rule and reign. You know my life from A to Z. You are the One who has placed passion in my heart for people, purpose and future. Guide my steps; allow Your magnetic power to draw me to my mission on the earth. I have tasted Your goodness and the things that drive my heart. I have learned to trust Your guidance. Like a shepherd, lead me to the desires of my heart and let me feast on Your word continuously. Only then is my heart for the King satisfied.
Amen

I declare I stand fully prepared to serve my King! I have influence to change the hearts of other to know my King. King Jesus is the way! I must boldly approach His throne to say, "If it pleases the King, I offer my heart." I have courage to say, "If I perish, I perish." I am willing to forsake my status, reputation and friends to follow Christ at any cost.

"Humility produces favor and identity; where entitlement forces favor and rights not earned."

God's Way vs. my way!

The greatest among you will be your servant. For whoever exalts himself will be humbled and whoever humbles himself will be exalted."

Matthew 23:11-12

ACTION STEPS:

✍ What does this mean to me?

✍ What must I do?

You

I feel so honored and blessed to know many of you who are loving the Lord and seeking to know how to serve Him more relationally and purposefully today! For those who attend classes in my home, and are so faithful to come and learn the ways of the Kingdom...I thank you! When I think of the 50 years or so that I have been filled with the Holy Spirit and mentoring women, I marvel that the Lord chose me. I seemed a very unlikely candidate, and yet...those are the ones He tends to choose. I am forever grateful. Of all the things I could have done with my life, the Lord opened my eyes to teach His Kingdom to women and mentor them to do the same! As well as mentor Kids at Camp, and develop a Kingdom mentality to the staff so that we function as God's Family and learn to become one in Christ! His grace and faithfulness has guided my path for all these years - how can I ever say thanks!

Enough about me, this is about you! I would like to remind you what God says about you and encourage you to believe it! My Christian life totally changed when I learned these truths and I began to see myself as God sees me. Talk about renewing of my mind, and being transformed to a brand new way of thinking! As you read through these wonderful truths, I challenge you to consider what

> "Your love has given me great joy and encouragement, because you, brother, have refreshed the hearts of the Lord's people" Philemon 1:7 NIV

each word says and stop and pray right then if you have doubts, unbelief, or question it! This is the difference between your own opinion, and the truth of how God sees you! The Holy Spirit is a comforter and teacher - allow His Spirit to lead you and guide you to a whole new mindset. In order to refresh the hearts of the Saints, (as mentioned in the above scripture in Philemon), you must be refreshed in order to have a desire to refresh others! You must believe the truth about who you are, and when you do, you will never be the same! God's Love for you is so awesome and vast that you find you cannot contain it; you must constantly give it away! Who does God say you are? And, as you refresh others, you are refreshed! You are standing in a beautiful valley with the Lord and He says to you with such love:

> "You are a sign and a wonder, a warrior born for this
> generation, you are filled with hope, joy, a future and
> purpose. Your destiny is fully awaiting you. You were
> born for such a time as this. You are brilliant because the
> light of Christ dwells in you. You are filled with My mercy
> and grace. You are a sheer delight to be around, you exude
> the love and fun that only I can bring. You stand in favor
> with Me and man. I make My appeal through you, you
> never grow tired or weary, My energy and strength are
> ever regenerating you; giving you the ability to soar like an
> eagle. My zeal and passion runs through your veins, and
> you never think of quitting! You have learned the art and

need for rest and give yourself permission to stop along the way and rest from your labor to give your body, mind and spirit time to re-align. You know the need to be in My presence and run there. You trust My word and choose to believe that when I speak, I only speak truth. You arise every morning ready to do business with Me and eager to know My mission for you for the day! You are filled with power and might; there is nothing you cannot do! My promise says, you can do all things through My power who lives within you. Health and well-being are changing your mind and body into a brand new creation. You are strong in the Lord and the power of His might! You have chosen to think the best of everyone instead of blaming and judging others realizing we are all in a growing pattern. God is not finished with you yet!

You strongly desire to obey Christ's commandment to:

> *"Go forth and make disciples of all nations, baptizing them in the name of the Father and of the Son and of the Holy Spirit, and teach them to obey everything I have commanded you. And remember, I am with you always, even unto the very end of the age!"*
> *Matthew 28:19-20 NIV*

Remember, we are called to make, teach, spend time with, encourage, and train disciples, not just make converts! That, too, but then converts must be discipled to learn the way of the Kingdom! As you have learned, it's not the way of the world, and not even the way of the church! It's a whole transformation of the way you think and accepting that it is not up to you, but Christ

who lives in you! He loved the Kingdom so much, He

came to earth to prove that
we could live in it with Him.
In fact, He said if we have
seen Him, we've seen the
Kingdom!

> *"I will sing of the Lord's great love forever; with my mouth I will make your faithfulness known through all generations. I will declare that your love stands firm forever, that you have established your faithfulness in heaven itself."*
> *Psalms 89:1-2*

How are you singing and

declaring His Love today? It

is time to sing and make melody in your hearts to the

Lord! Find at least one person today to share His Love

with.

> *"Sing to the Lord a new song; sing to the Lord, all the earth. Sing to the Lord, praise his name; proclaim his salvation day after day. Declare his glory among the nations, His marvelous deeds among all peoples."*
> *Psalms 96:1-3 NIV*

YOU are not ordinary! You are about to discover just how extraordinary you are. Did you ever think that having JESUS Living inside of you could be ordinary? No Way! It doesn't matter how young or old you are; or how much more time you have to live on the earth; You can finish Strong! Your latter days are promised to be greater than your former days. You desire to leave a strong legacy?

You are rising up to complete what God has started in you...Be known for something Wonderful to lift up the Name of Christ for your legacy! Now is the hour to ask of Him how to exalt His Name and how you can leave a great memory of your life with Him on earth. No greater way to be remembered than how you learned to LOVE!

ACTION STEPS:

✍ What does this mean to me?

✍ What must I do?

Zeal, Zealous

What do we do when we feel ourselves wilting, losing our fervor, or being disturbed because our prayers are not being answered? How do we handle being weary in well-doing, or allowing our flames to grow dim? Can we uncover the reason why we allowed this to happen? Do you think it's God's fault? Has He not been quick to tend to your broken heart when you called? Do you feel totally abandoned? Not only losing fellowship with the Lord but also friends as well? Does your heart border

> *"Never be lacking in ZEAL, but keep your spiritual fervor, serving the Lord!"*
> *Romans 12:11 NIV*

on being lukewarm? Then you probably do not want to read Revelation 3:15-21 as it is not a good finale! His Love is so constant, many times He allows our heart to become lonely because we are longing for more of Him!

He is calling us away for a hidden time to hear His voice for a brand new upgrade. This is a word to encourage you that He is Lord and is calling His Bride to be prepared before He comes for us! He wants to embrace and empower us to be all that is needed for the coming days! This is a glorious time to be invited into

> *"Don't burn out; keep yourselves fueled and aflame. Be alert servants of the Master, be cheerfully expectant. Don't quit in the hard times, pray even more!"*
> *Romans 12:11 MSG*

a more intimate time with Him and learn His ways. He is after our hearts! We might never have known we could be so in love and personally chosen, if He didn't beckon us to come away with Him

The Lord most assuredly knew this might happen, so He placed so many scriptures to help us along the way! I have always loved this one from John 10:10 (written by Rick Renner). I would like to share it with you:

> "The thief wants to get his hands into every good thing in your life. In fact, this pickpocket is looking for an opportunity to wiggle his way so deeply into your personal affairs that he can walk off with everything you hold precious and dear. And that's not all.... when he's finished stealing all your goods and possessions, he'll take his plan to rob you blind to the next level. He'll create conditions and situations so horrible that you'll see no way to solve the problem except to sacrifice everything that remains from his previous attacks. The goal of this thief is to totally waste and devastate your life. If nothing stops him, he'll leave you insolvent, flat broke, and cleaned out in every area of your life. You'll end up feeling as if you are finished and out of business! Make no mistake, the enemy's ultimate aim is to obliterate you..."(Rick Renner, Sparkling Gems from the Greek I, Tulsa, OK, 2003)

> *"But, I came that you might have, keep, and constantly retain a vitality, gusto, vigor, and zest for living that springs u from deep inside. I came that you might embrace this unrivaled, unequaled, matchless, incomparable, richly loaded and overflowing life to the ultimate maximum!"*
> *John 10:10 AMP*

So, how do we keep ourselves filled with spiritual fervor, and cheerfully expectancy, fueled, aflame, zealous, and never lacking in zeal? Three things

A Symphony of Words

are listed in the above scripture - don't quit, pray, and serve the Lord! May I offer a couple other things?

1. If you're dealing with unfulfilled expectations, and lost your trust in the Lord, (in fact you just may really be angry towards Him), then it's safe to say that you have lost your first love! That's not good! The results you won't be happy with! (Read Revelation 2:4). Repentance is a good thing....in fact it's absolutely necessary. Get over yourself and REPENT! God has His reasons for not answering your prayer at the moment you asked, and is calling on you to trust Him! He sees the bigger picture and knows that He is still at work on the answer, especially when other people are part of it.

2. You have possibly isolated yourself from the fellowship of others, prayer warriors, or those you know can help you through this lonely time. If you don't have a group like that, then for goodness sake, pray that the Lord will lead you to the right group! You are needing some TLC and for sure, a fresh touch from the Lord with

prayer, hugs, laughter, and possibly chocolate! (All are good)

3. It goes without saying, the Lord has been moved back into the shadows of your heart because He didn't meet your needs. He's not feeling welcome right now, and you need to be reminded that He has never left you abandoned, alone, nor forsaken. He is definitely there for you and most likely bidding you to:

"Come away My Beloved....let me kiss you with My Word, and hold you in my arms like a Shepherd tending a little lamb! You are My Beloved and I Am Yours, I Am with you, I Am in you, I have never left you, and I am calling you to a higher place (some call the Secret Place of the Highest). I want to show you great and mighty things which you have not known...I want to comfort your heart and remind you of My Love for you which never grows cold, not even lukewarm! I am working My plan for your life and bringing you to a place where My Spirit is alive and active - empowering you to be All that I created you to be! You are not left alone to figure it out, nor give up! My Word says, don't quit and I don't lie! You just watch what I will do...My plans are for good not evil! I am planning on a future and a hope for you.... don't stop now! You are almost to the victory line, and you win! My plan is to prosper you and bring great favor and blessing to you and yours! Better than any plan you could ever think of, dream of, or take a course on!"

There are so many other promises and assurances for us, but if you simply meditate on the above prophetic message, this truth will keep you busy repenting. And if you truly believe, then the truth will set you free and you will be back in the zeal camp...right back where you belong. Welcome to joy unspeakable full of His glory! Welcome to life overflowing, abundant, and filled with expectancy! Welcome joy back to a heart where laughter and fun just bubble over! Now you remember what hope looks like; something to live for. Zeal is contagious, so beware of friends who just want to hang out and suddenly your schedule is too full. You can't wait to get to your new group of Kingdom people who love worship, prayer, prophetic proclamations, and who can't get enough of Jesus and His Love! You know...the wierdos who used to embarrass you with their zeal & fervor. Before long, you are one of them - singing and dancing, praising and shouting, crying tears of joy for simply out of love for the presence of the Lord and each other! Yeah, it's called Kingdom - heaven on earth! Friends who are closer than family where the table is always open and set before you to, come and dine! It's time for celebration and fellowship with the Fam! Time to renew a right spirit and come alive once again with holy fervor, pure worship and rulership to your lonely heart. Ah yes, welcome home to the zeal camp! A little touch of Heaven's Kingdom on the Earth!

Love to all you ZEALOTS!

Prayer:
Father, my greatest desire for the reading of this book, is to bring hope, encouragement, joy and gladness. My purpose for this book is to incite action from the reader.
Amen

ZEALOUS is a powerful word! It can be powerful for good, or not so good. Depending upon what you are zealous about. In Bible days, Zealots were known as religious people who were overly passionate about their faith. It is one thing to be a Religious Zealot, but yet another to be totally in love with Jesus! Willing to live and die for Him and Serve Him with all your heart! If the fruit of the Spirit dwells and loves others through you, then your zeal can be contagious. If not, then you just might be known as a religious zealot who preaches the good news, but has not yet learned to live it! You are to be known by your fruits....Fruits of the Spirit are available to all who Believe and are filled with the Holy Spirit! But choosing to forsake our own carnal, selfish ways, is the proof of fruit that remains and will be delightfully tasty! Oh taste and see that the Lord is good!

ACTION STEPS:

✍ What does this mean to me?

✍ What must I do?

Ask yourself

- How can I apply this to my daily life?

- Who all can I share this book with to bring a change of heart, change of atmosphere or thinking?

- Why are letters of the alphabet important?

- What does it mean to me?

- What can I do with this information?

- What drew me to this book?

There are poems and stories using the letters and words in this book. Songs and melodies waiting to be sung. Listen closely and let the music begin – or let it continue...

"...be filled with the Spirit, speaking to one another with psalms, hymns, and songs from the Spirit. Sing and make music from your heart to the Lord, always giving thanks to God the Father for everything, in the name of our Lord Jesus Christ.
Ephesians 5:18-20

ABOUT THE AUTHOR

Shirley Ann Long Staires has always loved writing words, poems, letters and stories – which later turned into books. She often thought, "Wherever I am, would someone make sure I have a pen and paper!" Most of her life has been lived in Northeast Oklahoma and she calls Tulsa home (which is her favorite place to be). Regardless of extreme temperatures, hot and cold; plus storms and tornadoes, Oklahoma is the heartland of her existence. It is also the territory God has ordained for her ministry.

Shirley, Don and their four children moved to Avant, Oklahoma in 1982. Because of their love for influencing children to love Christ, Shepherd's Fold Summer Camp was established and continues to flourish today. To God be the glory! Her mentoring women classes are open to all women who are interested.

Shirley Staires can be contacted at shirleystaires@yahoo.com